83-413

Arthur M. Cohen

with

John Lombardi, Florence B. Brawer

assisted by
Joanne Frankel, Leslie Purdy
and the staff of the
ERIC Clearinghouse for Junior Colleges
University of California, Los Angeles

COLLEGE
RESPONSES
TO COMMUNITY
DEMANDS

Jossey-Bass Publishers
San Francisco • Washington • London • 1975

COLLEGE RESPONSES TO COMMUNITY DEMANDS
The Community College in Challenging Times
by Arthur M. Cohen and Associates

Address all inquiries to: Jossey-Bass, Inc., Publishers,
615 Montgomery Street, San Francisco, California 94111.

Library of Congress Catalogue Card Number LC 74-27912

International Standard Book Number ISBN 0-87589-252-3

Manufactured in the United States of America

JACKET DESIGN BY WILLI BAUM

FIRST EDITION

Code 7502

The Jossey-Bass
Series in Higher Education

A publication of the

EDUCATIONAL RESOURCES INFORMATION CENTER

Clearinghouse For Junior Colleges

UNIVERSITY OF CALIFORNIA, LOS ANGELES

*The ERIC program is sponsored by the
United States Department of Health, Education, and Welfare,
National Institute of Education.
The points of view expressed here do not necessarily represent
official National Institute of Education position or policy.*

Preface

National spokesmen for the community colleges repeatedly call for the colleges to become agents of community development. This change is to be effected by their providing quasi welfare services and coordinating the efforts of other educational agencies in their communities—in short, by their adopting a new mission that transcends the traditional function of providing academic and occupational education. Why are these calls for a redefinition of college purpose made? What do they mean?

To answer these questions, we, as analysts, search the literature, visit colleges, correspond with practitioners, talk with people seeking information, and listen, always listen, trying to understand how the colleges function. We are concerned with the magnitude of institutional change, the evolving role of college personnel, the college response to new social forces.

We report what we have learned in *College Responses to Community Demands*. This sequel to our previous work, *A Constant Variable* (Cohen and Associates, 1971), is intended for the same audience—administrators, trustees, counselors, and instructors in the colleges, university professors of higher education, and graduate students preparing to work in community colleges. Both books are critical analyses of the prevailing ideas and trends in two-year college education. Both presuppose the reader's familiarity with community college history, functions, and general operations.

In *A Constant Variable* we discussed the tensions within community colleges: their promise of equal opportunity without acceptance of responsibility for equal effects, and the conflict of their sorting and certifying function with the process of education. We concluded that much of this tension stems from a structure which precludes rapid change. Much also is a result of client perception—for each person who seeks something different from the college, twenty expect traditional services. And much can be ascribed to the people who operate the colleges and who, for better or worse, resist changing their work patterns.

College Responses to Community Demands extends this thesis. Here the tensions are described as external and internal pressures. The external pressures are societal forces such as state-level commissions and coordinating councils that mandate institutional roles, financial structures, and curriculum and instructional patterns. The internal forces are the preexisting institutional forms and the personal predilections of the staff and students. Our attention is directed toward the intersection of these pressures, the points where external forces meet internal counterpressures. Here, we feel, is a fruitful area for analyzing challenge and response, for assessing patterns of change in institutional functioning and in personal approach to the work role.

The subjects for discussion are drawn from recent developments affecting the colleges. Collective bargaining and affirmative action have advanced dramatically, the composition of the student body has changed, a trend toward requiring students to pay more of the costs of their own education is developing, and there is a tremendous oversupply of teaching personnel. Willingly or grudgingly, the colleges must adjust to all these forces.

College Responses to Community Demands is arranged

in three parts: Social Forces Intrude, Institutions Respond, and Faculty Persevere. We considered calling the first part The Camel Is in the Institutions' Tent All the Way Up to His Shoulders because the metaphor seems to fit the current situation. Gradually, steadily, seemingly irresistibly, governmental agencies, commissions, boards, and legislatures are impinging on the colleges. All is done with the best of intentions: program duplication among colleges in the same region must be avoided, data must be reported uniformly, minimum standards for programs and personnel must be maintained. But people in the colleges may be forgiven if they see the state as an unwelcome intruder. Pummeled by many rapidly shifting demands, they find it almost impossible to maintain their own vision of appropriate educational services.

Other outside forces intrude. Personnel selection processes are now determined down to the most minute detail by affirmative-action requirements. Collective bargaining agents negotiate conditions to which administrators and instructors must adhere. Tuition is imposed and the open door swings slowly toward the jamb.

In the first part of the book institutional adjustments to these and other forces are discussed. Chapter One provides an overview of external forces with some conclusions about why many educators find them attractive. Chapter Two examines current trends in collective bargaining and what they portend for college management. In Chapter Three rising tuition and fees are traced. And Chapter Four presents a review of affirmative action, particularly for women, raising some doubt about its immediate effect.

Another force, which threatens the institution as a whole, has arisen since 1972—the decline in the growth rate of enrollments. During the 1960s college planners acted in a fashion typical of both institutions and individuals—they bought into the bull market. While enrollments were growing, they expanded staff, buildings, and campuses without once considering the effect of a reversal of the enrollment trend. One searches in vain for evidence of contingency plans developed prior to 1972. It is as though planners expected the post–World War II baby boom to last forever, even though they could have learned otherwise merely by scanning census data.

In the second part of the book we describe several adjustments colleges have made in the face of shifting enrollment patterns. Chapter Five discusses reduction in force. Chapter Six offers examples of numerous specialized programs organized to attract new students. Chapter Seven presents a critique of attempts by the colleges to coordinate community services. Chapter Eight looks at experimental colleges as another response.

Not only the colleges but the people who work in them are periodically subject to new demands. As collective bargaining arrives, administrators are forced to become bureaucrats. Trustees' prerogatives diminish under the impact of state regulations. The faculty are supposed to be accountable and innovative at the same time they see their job security fading.

But not all the new pressures are negative. For faculty, particularly, a big change recently is that they are being regarded as human beings. Faculty retraining and reassignment programs are being initiated to counter the effects of reduction in force. Work satisfaction is discussed in administrative councils as presidents and deans become sensitive to the notion. Faculty contracts specify grievance procedures. And faculty development has become more than a synonym for the much-maligned in-service training program as numerous colleges plan genuine, long-term development programs.

In the third part we discuss who the faculty are, some of the demands placed on them, how they respond. Similarities and differences among instructors are traced and a new typology of innovativeness is presented in Chapter Nine. Chapter Ten offers the results of studies of work satisfaction, relating satisfaction to professionalism in teaching. The idea that staff evaluation can be useful in promoting personal and professional development is defined in Chapter Eleven.

Chapter Twelve discusses the function of the community college and the contradictions between it and the "new mission" of colleges as agents of community development.

A few of our biases should be stated at the outset. A general belief shaping our work is that the American community college lacks a coherent philosophy. The guiding principle that the colleges should offer something for everyone, everywhere, anytime provides no foundation for sequential curriculum or instructional forms of demonstrable efficacy.

We believe that an educational institution needs a large percentage of self-aware staff members. The institution has a responsibility to foster personal integration and awareness among all its employees. We also have faith in collegiality as an ideal even though we recognize that it is fading rapidly in practice. The best we can anticipate is that the individual administrator or instructor will be able to maintain his professional balance despite the impending storm of adversary relationships among contending groups.

We deplore the debasement of the liberating arts within the colleges at a time when their clients need guidance in personally profitable leisure-time pursuits. Correspondingly we question the emphasis on manpower training, which in many respects is little more than credentialism. If labor unions and leaders of business and industry decide to provide apprenticeship training without using the college as a coordinating agency, colleges will find it difficult to return to the liberal arts. They may then relive the history of the secondary schools.

We deplore staff members' refusal to attend to the discipline of teaching. But for a few, faculty members are not learning how to teach capably, and, with rare exception, college administrators fail to hold themselves accountable for instructional effects. Accordingly, we believe that the community college today might well be described in terms formerly reserved for motion picture theaters, museums, parks, and public libraries. Although any individual client may achieve illumination, nothing more is promised to the community as a whole than that the opportunity is present. Offering this opportunity is the staff's distinct contribution. Avoiding responsibility for program effects is its major failing.

Los Angeles   ERIC Clearinghouse for Junior Colleges
January 1975   ARTHUR M. COHEN, Director

Contents

THREE: FACULTY PERSEVERE

Authors

FLORENCE B. BRAWER is a research psychologist in the ERIC Clearinghouse for Junior Colleges. Associate editor of *New Directions for Community Colleges* and a former community college psychometrist and counselor, her special interest in personality assessment of people in higher education led to her previously published book, *New Perspectives on Personality Development in College Students*. She prepared the chapter on affirmative action in this book and coauthored the chapters on the experimental college, the faculty, and faculty development.

ARTHUR M. COHEN is associate professor of higher education at the University of California, Los Angeles, director of the Clearinghouse, and editor-in-chief of *New Directions for Community Colleges*. He has written extensively on two-year college faculty, curriculum, and instruction. His previously published works include *Dateline '79: Heretical Concepts for the Community*

College and the award-winning *Confronting Identity: The Community College Instructor,* coauthored with Florence B. Brawer. He conceived and edited this book, wrote the chapters on state influence, community development, job satisfaction, and open enrollment, and collaborated on the chapters dealing with the experimental college and faculty development.

JOANNE FRANKEL is a research associate at the Clearinghouse, and she has taught in the Los Angeles City Schools. She wrote the chapter on expanding the market.

JOHN LOMBARDI is a continuing consultant with the Clearinghouse and an examiner for the Commission on Institutions of Higher Education of the North Central Association of Colleges and Secondary Schools. He has served as president of Los Angeles City College and as assistant superintendent in charge of Los Angeles community colleges. His widespread interests are reflected in his chapters on collective bargaining, tuition, and reduction in force.

LESLIE PURDY, assistant research educationist in the Clearinghouse, is a former student counselor and dean of students. A portion of the chapter on faculty is based on a participant observation study she conducted at a community college in Southern California.

The staff of the ERIC Clearinghouse for Junior Colleges under Marcia Boyer, associate director, prepared the manuscript. Janet Bloom, senior editor, compiled the Bibliography.

College Responses
to Community Demands

The Community College
in Challenging Times

Chapter One

State Influence Grows

Control of community colleges is gravitating toward state capitals. Responsibility for funding, planning, and managing everything from cost accounting to instructional techniques is moving steadily away from local officials. An increasing portion of financial support comes from the state, and state agencies distribute most of the federal funds to the colleges. Statewide information networks are frequently seen, along with staff development, funded by the state and with guidelines evolved at the state level. Faculty groups, administrators, and trustees now maintain their own lobbyists in the legislature and insist on being represented on decision-making bodies. Since 1960, nearly half the states have established community college boards. And there is a definite trend toward coordination of all higher education in each state through postsecondary commissions.

Many community college administrators applaud this tendency toward large-scale coordination for minimizing duplication of effort and maximizing acquisition of funds to support well-orchestrated programs. But such coordination has other consequences not often traced or anticipated. The role of

1

people in the colleges shifts markedly as coordination (not control, the apologists hasten to affirm) becomes a statewide matter, and patterns of curriculum and instruction alter as the manner of deciding what shall be offered changes.

In determining the courses to be offered, state-level influences create pressures on the colleges, some direct, others not. The legislature exerts the most direct influence, followed by the state community college board, various licensing agencies and commissions, and professional associations.

State education codes as formulated by the legislature frequently spell out not only what courses must be given but the content of each course. According to the California code, social science courses must include "a study of the role, participation, and contribution of black Americans, American Indians, Mexicans, persons of oriental extraction, and other ethnic groups to the economic, political, and social development of California and the United States of America" (1971, Sec. 25516.3). More often the codes require particular course patterns but leave the specific details to the state board.

States also encourage certain courses through funding. For example, vocational education is often funded at a higher rate than are academic programs, and additional funds are provided for remedial programs and disadvantaged students. States can discourage certain programs by not funding them; hobby courses are typically required to be self-supporting, and courses requested by commercial companies often have to be partially funded by the company obtaining the trained employees.

The pattern of reimbursement also has direct influence on the college program. The California average daily attendance formula reimburses the district on the basis of weekly student-contact hours. Michigan combines the size of enrollment with certain program criteria and varies the amount of reimbursement according to the size of the college. Ohio and Colorado give differential support to occupational, academic, and general programs. New York provides special assistance to colleges enrolling sizable proportions of disadvantaged students.

The postsecondary education commissions in many states have an impact too. Designed to coordinate all higher education, they include representatives from both public and private universities and colleges, along with proprietary schools, various other state education agencies, and the general public. The California commission, for example, is empowered to conduct studies of need (individual, program, community, curriculum), review proposals for new programs, develop criteria for evaluating college effectiveness, and "require the segments to submit data on plans, programs, and policy development," both short and long range, "in a form specified by the Commission" ("New California Postsecondary Education Commission . . . ," 1974, p. 133).

State community college boards influence curriculum and instruction through course approvals and other procedures. The Colorado board has divided the state into major planning areas for allocating occupational curriculums. (Some areas are authorized to offer cattle-ranching; others, ski-lodge maintenance.) And along with many other state boards it has adopted a mode of fiscal accounting that ties institutional budgets to program functions and eventually to instructional objectives in curriculum planning.

State governing boards show considerable diversity in their activities; however, some generalizations can be made. A study done by Wattenbarger and Sakaguchi (1971) shows how boards assume primary roles in developing master plans and standards for establishing new colleges, recommending budgets to the legislature, and establishing fee patterns and how they play secondary roles in developing new educational programs and policies affecting students. The study concludes that grading policies and faculty appointment, promotion, and tenure procedures are left to the colleges. However, there is considerable variance nationwide, and some state boards exercise much control, establishing academic standards for graduation, student probation, dismissal, and readmission. The board of governors of the California community colleges reviews academic master plans for each district, passes on interdistrict agreements for special classes, and establishes precise criteria for graded and nongraded classes. Specific guidelines and review procedures for staff development in Florida colleges are maintained through the state board.

Many states have commissions for teacher preparation and licensing, which operate separately from other state boards or agencies. These groups develop and maintain standards and procedures for instructor certification, approve pre- and in-service teacher preparation patterns, and develop procedures for evaluation of teacher performance. They also recommend legislation affecting teacher certification.

The requirements for teacher certification affect the educational program of the college by screening out certain people. Frequently state education codes require a loyalty oath and knowledge of the United States Constitution (as evidenced by having taken a course). Credentials may be denied because of felony convictions, debilitating physical handicaps, and addiction to alcohol or drugs. The applicant must also swear he has never engaged in any act involving moral turpitude. But licensing commissions are susceptible to pressure from a variety of organized groups, and the California code now contains a proviso that a person may not be denied a credential or employment because he is partially or totally blind.

Professional associations, including unions, exert state-level influence in a variety of ways. Since the inception of community colleges there has been a variety of such associations: groups composed of a cross-section of concerned people who purport to speak for the community colleges with one voice, groups comprised exclusively of presidents or trustees or faculty members, and groups speaking for special interests within the institution, such as vocational-technical faculty associations. Professional associations prepare position papers for distribution to state boards and legislative committees and frequently lobby directly. They perform a variety of other services including publication of newsletters, sponsorship of conferences, and operation of placement or teacher exchange services statewide.

Faculty professional associations have gained direct influence through negotiation of contracts. In Ohio, Minnesota, and New York, statewide faculty contracts, which specify hours an employee may work, duties that may be assigned to him, conditions for appointment, and most other aspects of the instructor's work life, are negotiated by the representative faculty association, and, according to the 1973 Minnesota agreement, the faculty association may meet with the state junior college board at least three times a year to present association views on any matter considered significant by either the board or the association.

The state university impinges on community colleges in numerous ways. The most direct effects come through course approvals and transfer requirements—situations where the university must approve a particular course or a set of courses for transfer.

The administrative and faculty training programs conducted in the universities have less influence than professional associations. If the leaders of these programs have a well-defined vision of what community colleges should be like, if they are vigorous in their recruiting efforts, and if they interact frequently with the practitioners in the colleges, the programs may determine the pattern of development of community colleges in the state. But when university community college programs are not clearly defined and are run simply as adjuncts to training programs for other levels of education, this aspect of university influence diminishes.

All these boards, agencies, and associations impinge on the colleges; they also impinge on each other. As each group becomes more unified, the potential for collision among groups is greater. Conflict between well-organized faculty groups and local and state governing boards, once unthinkable, has become common. Some of the issues are power disputes, such as who sets teacher certification requirements. Others are substantive, concerning such issues as extra pay for certain work.

All the issues and the ways they are settled have an effect on the people involved. As the institutions with which they are affiliated become a state system, trustees and administrators forget how to be educational leaders. This change in their role is subtle, insidious. Gradually, they become concerned not with what programs are best offered but with how to manipulate the funding formulas to maximize the flow of dollars into the insti-

tution. Saddest of all, the students are denied the opportunity
to see intelligent people making decisions independently. This
is the result in the elementary and secondary schools. It is
happening now in the junior colleges.

The example afforded by the lower schools is instructive.
Local public school administrators have operated under stringent state-level guidelines for more than a generation, and they
have developed an appropriate working method: they seek to
interpret regulations and code books, not to make original
plans. Today, few public schools have anyone on their staff
who knows how to do a study of curriculum or instruction.
What are the philosophical bases of alternative curriculum
plans? What students should be served and in what way? What
information must be collected? It would not occur to a public
school principal to ask these questions, and if it did he would
not know where to begin.

For evidence of this effect in the two-year colleges, scan
the minutes or summary statements of statewide meetings of
presidents, deans, and other administrative subgroups to see
whether they talk now about the same things they did ten or
twenty years ago. Some marked changes are apparent even in
the few years that the fifty Southern California junior college
deans of instruction have been meeting together. They used to
consider courses and instruction at their own colleges; now
they discuss which state agency has the final say on what program or which division requires what data. As Shawl (1974)
points out, their personal style—their perception of how they
are supposed to conduct their daily affairs, of what they should
be concerned with—has changed. They perceive fewer options,
feeling that decisions about their instructional programs are
made elsewhere. Most notably, they seem quite comfortable
with their position in a bureaucratic network that reaches from
the state capital through their district superintendent's office
and into and around their own desks.

The preconception of what it means to be a college dean
or president is affected as well. Graduate students seeking certification for top administrative posts learn about state-level
agencies, how they operate, whom they represent, what powers

they have. The few students who read educational philosophy do so as an adjunct to their professional preparation, not as a central part of it. Most do not perceive the considered formulation of their own value positions as necessary or even useful. Why would anyone seek to understand educational philosophy when one knows that the state education code is the Bible? The obvious answer is that the routine functions of a bureaucracy require no special training. Any—or no—field of study prepares a person to learn the rules.

State-level forces affect instructors, too. The general faculty response to centralized planning is to demand more and more control over matters of less and less importance. Fringe benefits become crucial points for arbitration; curriculum planning fails to make the agenda. And to the individual instructor, bureaucracy is bureaucracy. The restrictions that bind his actions—the number of students he may have, the courses he may teach, how he may teach them—are negotiated by his elected representatives. More and more, state-level influences are forcing him into a new role. If he is sufficiently concerned with his work, he defines precise instructional outcomes and collects evidence of his own effects. The less vigorous instructor shies away from this activity and accepts a role as factotum performing on behalf of absentee curriculum makers.

In self-defense each group of practitioners organizes so that their collective voice can be heard where decisions are made. The call for one statewide formal organization of deans of instruction states in part, "If we are to remain effective educational leaders, the time to be heard is NOW. With the current trends this may be our last chance before we are relegated to counting chairs and checking attendance." But this is the cry of a group; each individual within it has abandoned whatever dream he had of gathering information on student preferences, weighing it against his own carefully nurtured philosophy of education, and fostering curriculum at his own institution.

Nevertheless, people are not totally uninvolved. Individual options become fewer as the code books grow thicker, but there is no such thing as a faceless bureaucrat. Someone, some small group must make the fine choices about the curriculum, instruction, and other services to be provided within the defined limits. And someone must translate the decision into action. For convenience we continually attempt to anthropomorphize our institutions, saying, "The college decided to . . . ," but people stand behind all decisions and actions.

People create the variations found in all colleges—variations that do not merely reflect a difference in codes or environment. A strong business program in one institution, an outstanding remedial program in another, have little to do with state codes or the community in which the college is located.

For example, in the Modesto Junior College (California) agricultural program every student has a paid job in a local dairy, packing house, or other agricultural business. Why there? Is it because that college is in the heart of an agricultural area? Imperial Valley College (California), which sits in the middle of thousands of acres of lettuce, onions, alfalfa, and carrots, has an agricultural program hardly worth mentioning. But that college is a leader in American Indian archaeology, with its own carbon-dating equipment and students working in digs all around the valley perimeter. Mount Hood Community College (Oregon) has an exceedingly well-developed fine arts program with separate buildings for sculpture, graphics, textiles, and ceramics, and with more students studying and performing music than in most colleges three times its size. El Camino College, in a suburb of Los Angeles, has a professional concert and dance series that is the envy of other communities. Why? Are there no opportunities in Los Angeles for people to attend professional recitals? One cannot understand such program development merely by saying that it is a good idea to have agriculture, archaeology, fine arts, or public concerts in community colleges; one must look to the people. Each of the colleges mentioned has an exceptionally vigorous program director who has taken it on himself to build his own division. In the face of any system, man insists on holding up his head.

Considering the influences exerted on community colleges and their response so far, is the move toward greater state influence positive or negative? It depends on one's values, on what one sees as the major institutional function and the role

of each individual within the institution. The potential benefits and dangers of statewide influence have been speculated on
for many years. The dangers are usually listed as homogeniza-
tion (all institutions doing essentially the same thing), a break-
down in local control and consequent unresponsiveness to the
community, and a general tendency toward bureaucratism or
institutionalization that diminishes individuality. Benefits are
frequently listed as stable funding (which allows for long-range
program planning), coordination of institutions with the economies attendant upon avoidance of program duplication, and
all-around institutional upgrading through the setting of minimum operational standards.

It is difficult to obtain useful data on these general
effects. Does pluralism diminish, for example, as state-level
influences become greater? Such causal connections cannot be
readily established. State-level influences have always operated
to some degree, hence we have no antecedent group of community colleges with which we can compare the present-day
institutions. There is some indication, however, that colleges
become more alike as state-level influences become more pronounced. The pattern seems to be that of the secondary schools,
which arose indigenously, then were put under state authoriza-
tion. As more money was obtained from the state than locally,
final approval of courses of study and other institutional operations shifted from the local districts to the state board. Today
we have essentially one secondary school curriculum in each
state with minimal variation between districts. The problem in
attributing the similarity between schools to increased state-
level influence or control is that the ideas undergirding secondary schools are common across the country. A similar case
prevails for community colleges—when one is established, its
statement of purpose, intent, and philosophy is typically indis-
tinguishable from that of others throughout the state or indeed
anywhere in the nation. Accordingly its pattern of operation is
markedly similar.

Does centralization diminish the community-centered-
ness of the two-year college? J. Peterson (1969) reports a study of
two community colleges, one under state control in Massachu-

setts and one under local control in New York. He concludes
that there is no difference between these two institutions in
their relations with their local communities. Their curriculums
are similar. The locally controlled college is more adaptable
than the other, but the difference is not as decisive as might
be expected. Undoubtedly Peterson's assertion needs further
study since it tends to refute common sense speculation.

Gleazer (1974b) pleads for the community colleges to
become more community centered and to respond quickly to
community needs through better recruitment of students, use
of local advisory committees, and cooperation with other educational agencies. He also reports local apprehension that state-
level boards might decrease community orientation and the
capacity to respond easily and quickly to local needs. But are
local boards invariably responsive to community needs? How
many districts would still be running racially separate and
unequal two-year colleges if local option were paramount? In
the early 1970s the national administration was enamored of
revenue sharing—remitting funds to local governments osten-
sibly because they are responsive to social needs in their areas.
But much of this money runs into the same old channels—law
enforcement, fire protection, and street repair—not to social
services. College boards of trustees are no more socially aware
than are boards of county supervisors.

The move toward state-mandated processes is not a move
toward rational planning, theory-based decisions, coherent philosophy, or consistent value positions. But neither is it a move
away from all this. Its main effect is in switching the pressure
of groups and influential individuals to a larger arena—from the
campus to the state capitol. Do the colleges boost intelligence?
Do they affect social standing or promote egalitarianism? Do
they raise income level or develop personality? Or, simply, do
students like the programs? State-level data collection is used
almost exclusively to support predetermined conclusions, not
to shed light on these questions.

The persistent failure to assess college impact or to adhere to consistent value positions makes it impossible to determine how any single change relates to a total plan. If no one

provides evidence that one curriculum or instructional pattern has a greater effect than another on the life of individual students or on the community the college serves, then decisions are made on the basis of political persuasion, the whim of a legislator, the skill of a canny parliamentarian in a commission meeting, or the vociferousness of a bloc leader in a board room.

Grande and Singer (1970) surveyed a large group of college administrators who overwhelmingly commend the drift toward state-level coordination and control. We suggest that the reason for their support is institutional survival. Statewide coordination promises to enhance the life span of even the most labile colleges by preserving their monopoly in certain areas. Competition is a bugbear to community colleges. Watkins (1973, p. 2) points out that "one- and two-year programs, formerly the province of proprietary schools and the community and junior colleges, are proliferating in four-year institutions. Forty percent of the American Association of State Colleges and Universities' 370 member institutions now offer 'less-than bachelor's' programs." How to keep these other institutions out? Glenny (1974) says, "Community colleges will look to the state coordinating agency (and quite possibly to the legislature) to control or prevent [state colleges' starting new associate degree programs]. . . . A still more serious problem in program competition is . . . that a host of additional institutions are attempting to invade the adult education market. . . . At least one likely outcome of . . . state intervention will be protection of . . . community colleges" (pp. 56–57).

We are not deprecating the idea of state community college boards or that of coordinating boards for all higher education; we are merely speculating why so many community college leaders find them attractive. Educators certainly have the prerogative of feeling that decisions about their programs are better made elsewhere. If so, we applaud their honesty while deploring their lack of professionalism. However, the truth seems to be that educators are grasping at anything that promises to help them keep their institutions afloat. The acceleration of this trend will result in the continuing decline in public esteem for education and, consequently, in ready access to the public treasury.

Chapter Two

Collective Bargaining Impinges on Management

After a slow start in the 1960s collective bargaining is making headway faster in the community colleges than in any other segment of higher education. By the middle of 1974 more than two hundred colleges in eighteen states and the District of Columbia were covered by collective bargaining agreements. If states with collective negotiation, that is, so-called "meet and confer" laws, were included, these numbers would double. Collective bargaining contracts cover all colleges in Minnesota, Hawaii, the State University of New York system, New York City, and Chicago; all but one of the twenty-nine colleges in Michigan; all but one of the twenty-seven Washington colleges; all but two of the fifteen colleges in New Jersey; and a large portion of the colleges in Illinois and Wisconsin ("Where College Faculties . . . ," 1974).

The number of colleges covered by agreements will certainly increase as more states enact legislation giving faculty the right to negotiate. In 1973, Oregon passed a bill permitting collective bargaining, and a similar bill passed the California legislature but was vetoed by the governor. By 1980 half the colleges in the nation will be engaged in collective bargaining; 60 to 75 percent of the faculty will be covered by contracts. Further, although formal written contracts are not legal in many states, local boards in effect engage in bargaining, and their policy manuals include many topics found in collective bargaining agreements. To stave off collective bargaining, some boards match the salaries, workloads, and fringe benefits included in contracts in neighboring colleges. The Education Commission of the States suggests that bargained agreements tend to set the pace in salary and working conditions (*Faculty Collective Bargaining* . . . , 1972).

Despite this pattern, collective bargaining is not inevitable in every college; it is far from universal in *any* enterprise. Some faculties are so satisfied with their working conditions that they resist collective bargaining; others are ideologically opposed to the adversary labor-management concept; others are in colleges with such a high faculty turnover that unionization is impractical; and still others are in states or colleges where organization for collective bargaining is prohibited, discouraged, or repressed. Nevertheless, trustees and administrators would be negligent if they failed to plan for collective bargaining. Since the initiative to invoke collective bargaining remains with the faculty, the administration may not be able to inhibit the pace (*Faculty Collective Bargaining* . . . , 1972). Pertinent also is the possibility of judicial action, such as the Florida Supreme Court ruling that public employees have an absolute right to collective bargaining under the state constitution, or federal action requiring compliance with collective bargaining (*Current,* 1973), especially as a condition of participation in federal aid programs (House Report 9730 and House Report 8677, National Public Employment Relations Act of 1973). In individual colleges, trustees and chief administrators who consider collective bargaining incompatible with the purposes and operation of a college may still have the option to create an environment that would lead faculty and other employees to eschew collective bargaining. But they should not count on it too strongly.

Data collected from 951 full-time faculty members in

ten Pennsylvania community colleges suggest that a majority
are favorably disposed to both faculty organization and collective negotiation (Moore, 1970). Within faculty ranks some
discussion exists "concerning the desirability of various coercive
tactics. Certain forms of sanctions generally are viewed as ethical actions to be used by faculty in the face of an impasse. However, there is considerable disagreement concerning the ap-
propriateness of work stoppages as a collective tactic" (p. 40).
Those instructors who express positive attitudes to collective
bargaining look on themselves as relatively mobile. Interest-
ingly, they demonstrate a drive toward increased faculty power
because they indicate a "low sense of power," and feel themselves "relatively incapable of influencing the course of events
within their college" (p. 42).

Kennelly's (1972) review of collective bargaining across
the United States compares a number of institutions in terms
of extent of faculty collective bargaining, trends in collective
negotiations, and collective bargaining as a locus of decision-
making in academic governance. Three conceptual models of
collective bargaining are presented, and findings from the
survey of 273 faculty members in 191 institutions suggest that
while only 29 percent report collective bargaining, the greatest
incidence is in community colleges. Fifty percent of the community colleges, compared with 24 percent of the universities,
report bargaining activity.

As in any other collective bargaining, contracts for community colleges are negotiated between two parties—the employees and the employers. It may appear supererogatory to
discuss the nature or the composition of the negotiating prin-
cipals—the faculty, as represented by an organization of their
choice, and the board of trustees or its representatives (the
president, business manager, labor negotiator, and so on). But
local practices, state laws, and national and state labor relations board rulings are changing this simple definition of bargaining agents. Within and among states there are variations
on the nature and composition of the bargaining units.

The unit may be a single college, a multicampus or
multicollege district, or a statewide system of colleges. It may

include only community colleges or all segments of higher education. The most common is the single college unit. Multicampus districts are invariably organized in one unit, although there has been some discussion in the state of Washington to permit each college in a multicampus unit to bargain individually (*Collective Bargaining/Professional Negotiations*, 1973).

In Hawaii a proposed agreement for 1973–1976 specifies one unit for the faculty of the University of Hawaii and the community college system. Nonfaculty personnel are provided for in a different unit. Similarly, in Minnesota all community colleges are included in one unit (1973). New York State has three basic variations: locally controlled community colleges have individual or multicampus units; those controlled by the State University of New York (SUNY), including the two-year institutions known as technical institutes, are in another unit; and all colleges in the City University of New York (CUNY) system comprise still another unit.

The employee bargaining unit may be an independent faculty association, an affiliate of one of three national organizations—American Association of University Professors (AAUP), the American Federation of Teachers (AFT) (AFL-CIO), the National Education Association (NEA)—a united AFT-NEA affiliate, or a consortium of three or more organizations, including one or more representing nonclassroom employees. The employee unit of CUNY, for example, is composed of an alliance of unions and NEA affiliates known as the Professional Staff Congress, and that of SUNY is the United University Professionals (NEA/AFT).

Full-time classroom instructors comprise the core of the employee bargaining unit, but other nonclassroom groups and part-time instructors are being included with increasing frequency. The most common additions are counselors, librarians, and curriculum specialists. The expansion of categories for inclusion in the employee bargaining unit is a result of the organization's need to increase its influence by incorporating as many key personnel as possible; get the dues to employ an executive secretary, retain a lawyer, accountant, professional negotiator, and other support personnel as required, and build a war chest in case of prolonged strike; and obviate the assignment of nonprofessional employees to classes during a strike. The inclusion of nonteaching professionals is most marked in the CUNY (1973) and SUNY (1971) contracts.

The employer bargaining unit is usually a local or state community college governing board or a city or state governing board of higher education, but it may be a noneducational governing board. In New York State a county may be the employer bargaining unit if the county government sponsors the community college, although in practice representatives of the college board of trustees have a major voice in the negotiations (McHugh and O'Sullivan, 1971). Technically, in some contracts the state, represented by the governor, is the employer unit.

The employer bargaining unit rather than a group of individuals within the unit represents the public interest. This team is directed by the chief executive officer of the governing unit—a superintendent, chancellor, or university president. In most negotiations he is represented by specialists, including a small number of administrators.

The employer-employee relationship introduced by collective bargaining changes the collegial governance pattern, which has been characterized by the AAUP position that a faculty member is an officer of his institution rather than a hired employee and the North Central Association Commission on Institutions of Higher Education position that "the faculty personnel of an institution are not regarded as employees occupying designated positions in a hierarchy" (Campbell, 1974, p. 26).

In the new relationship the faculty give up the right to deal with the administrators on an individual basis and are prevented from initiating changes in methods of instruction or curriculum except after consultation with the bargaining agent. As individuals they come under the jurisdiction of a second bureaucracy—the association or union. Where the agency shop is legal, their right to work depends on membership in or support of the bargaining unit, whether or not they agree with its principles. In return, faculty gain the protection of an independent organization (often affiliated with a state and national organization), freedom from arbitrary action, greater control over their working conditions, and a larger share in policy determination.

For the employer unit a basic question arises: "Is there really a management function in a college or university that specifically is borne by the administration and board?" Posed by an advisory committee of the Education Commission of the States and by administrators (personal communication with R. Camphire, Nov. 1973), this question not only reflects doubt that there is such a function but also indicates the strong hold collegiality has on college and university people. The employer unit has difficulty reconciling collegiality with an adversary relationship. Collective bargaining, however, is forcing it to address this issue (Schneider, 1974).

Whether or not a management function concept is developed and exercised depends on the skill of employer negotiators at the bargaining table. They must counter a strong drive by employee negotiators for the continuance of many practices developed under collegiality or participatory democracy. The position of AFT has been explicitly stated over the past ten years. Illustrative is the opinion of the Executive Secretary of the California State Federation of Teachers that "two groups in higher education make policy: the board and the faculty. It is the function of administration to implement policy, not to make it. A good administrator under such a system is the servant of the faculty and not its director. He executes policy as it is formulated" (Schloming, 1963, p. 2).

Ten years later President Israel Kugler of the New York State AFT College and University Council presented to the New York Public Employment Relations Board about thirty-five negotiable issues including economic issues and many academic ones, such as "consultation on educational matters, curriculum admissions, student activities, choice of administrators including deans, chairmen, and presidents, . . . master plan formulation, educational policy governing the entire university, establishment of new campuses, . . . and finally, but not least, selection of the chancellor and other central administrators" (McHugh, 1973, pp. 42–43). The NEA and AAUP positions are in principle less extreme but in practice quite similar to that of the AFT. If the board and the employee unit are the policy makers, the administrators become ministerial officers. In the extreme position announced by Schloming even the chief executive officer—the superintendent, chancellor, or president—is excluded from policy-making (Chandler and Chiang, 1973).

Two studies, one on faculty workload (Lombardi, forthcoming a) and the other on reduction in force (RIF) (Lombardi, forthcoming b), show the extent to which collective bargaining agreements circumscribe the prerogatives of management. In most agreements hours of work, class size, utilization of free time, and compensation for overload assignments are minutely described. To a lesser extent sections on RIF are also detailed. Similar observations can be made about salaries, grievance procedures, job security, and faculty evaluation.

Another issue relating to management is the insistence of the faculty leaders that the chief executive and representatives of the board of trustees meet at the bargaining table as a sign of respect for the faculty and good faith in the bargaining process (Shaw and Clark, 1972). This demand is essentially an effort by the employee group to influence the selection of the employer negotiators in order to bargain with the least qualified members. If successful it would undermine the independence of the employer group and contravene its adversary nature.

Allied with this are the inroads the faculty unit makes on the selection of management personnel. As Kugler states, the AFT considers the selection of all administrators to be negotiable. This position conforms to the practice in many colleges before the advent of collective bargaining, when collegiality prevailed and faculty were considered to be officers of the college rather than employees of the board. Although the AFT, NEA, and AAUP now accept the adversary relationship basic to collective bargaining, they do not want to give up all elements of collegiality.

Alert to the consequences of this issue, a few board members and administrators are insisting on their right to appoint management personnel, but most agreements in community colleges, voluntarily or by virtue of concessions in bargaining, permit considerable faculty participation in the selection of such personnel. It is common to have faculty representation on selection committees for all positions, especially department and division heads.

In the selection of members of governing boards, faculty, through their local and state organizations, often recommend particular candidates to the appointing official (mayor, supervisor, governor) or support individuals running for elected positions. When successful in gaining a majority of board members favorably disposed to the faculty, their representatives at the bargaining table gain significant concessions from the employer negotiators. This process is available to trustees and administrators, but in elections they do not have the influence that the larger faculty group enjoys.

The power of administrators is further diminished by a change in the relationships among the board, the chancellor, the president, deans, and other administrators. Collective bargaining brings to light and exacerbates a conflict between the board and superintendent on one side and various administrators on the other.

The assumption that these officers have a common interest because they are administrators is not, nor was it ever, warranted. The board and the chancellor or chief administrative officer have a common purpose for the obvious reason that the chief administrative officer represents the board and must be responsive to board wishes. But the other administrators are not so closely bound up with the board and the chancellor. They are employees just as the faculty and other nonadministrative employees are.

A conflict has existed for a long time, but its consequences were not serious when the colleges were small and multicampus systems were not so numerous. Large size, red tape, and growth of large central office staffs lead to the central office versus campus syndrome and the tendency of each administrator to build his own empire. Moreover, in the large colleges and multicampus systems the superintendent or chancellor often becomes an institutional executive rather than an educational administrator and leader. The distance between him and the classroom widens to chasmlike proportions. His chief concerns are with the budget, the legislature, collective bargaining, and public relations. The chief administrator tends to become authoritarian and insensitive to the views and concerns of the administrators who carry out the day-to-day operations of the college. Chief administrators organize committees for developing policies and guidelines, but these are often seen as sops that give the semblance of group participation. Rarely do committee recommendations truly represent the views of those campus administrators who will not openly and vigorously oppose the chief administrator's point of view. Such opposition would raise doubts about loyalty and harmony.

Collective bargaining also induces a change of relationships among administrators. Only a few administrators participate directly in the negotiating process. Some colleges have prenegotiation strategy meetings that enable administrators to express their views; they even prepare a priority list of items in which the administrators have a stake. This is a viable procedure in single campus districts, but in multicampus districts it is at best cumbersome. In neither case can the inputs of administrators who are not on the employer negotiating team be decisive at the bargaining table. Such administrators act sometimes through representatives selected as resource persons for the negotiators. In general, administrator influence on the negotiations varies inversely with the number of campuses involved.

Contracts may affect not only the responsibilities of administrators but their prerogatives, salaries, fringe benefits, and tenure. The implementation of many of the contractual provisions falls upon administrators from deans to chairmen. They must live with the agreement for the duration of the contract, which extends up to three years. Under extreme circumstances administrators can ask the employer negotiators to reopen negotiations on a specific section, but this option, where it exists, is not frequently used. By and large, the administrators are left in limbo (Salmon, 1972).

Collective bargaining need not destroy the management function, but it hardly strengthens it. The possibility also exists for cooperation between the faculty and the administrative employee groups. Although a seemingly farfetched idea (but less so than strikes were ten years ago) the administrators might even refuse to cross a picket line during a faculty strike.

All this points up the absence of a management concept of administration. The efforts of some presidents to introduce management through objectives, program-planning-budget systems, management information systems, and other practices borrowed from business, indicate an awareness of this deficiency. Much more progress needs to be made though—and soon—if the management function is to remain with the board and administrators and if the slight stirrings toward collective bargaining for administrators are not to become a ferment comparable to that of faculty bargaining. Chief administrators in large colleges and in multicampus districts must not become more directive and less sensitive to the views and concerns of the campus administrators. They must develop in-service management programs and create incentives for excellent performance. For example, administrative salaries and benefits should be independent of faculty salaries; the common practice of tying administrative salaries to faculty salaries makes administrators dependent on the success of the employees at the bargaining table. Already a half dozen or more college boards in Michigan (*Policies and Procedures . . .* , 1973) and New York (McHugh and O'Sullivan, 1971) have entered into agreements with the administrators not classified as executive officers.

At the employer-employee bargaining level boards of trustees and chief administrators must match the expert faculty negotiating team. The general opinion is that employers need experienced labor relations personnel to do the negotiating and to monitor the implementation of contract terms. There is near unanimity in feeling that the chief executive and members of the board are not qualified nor do they have the time to act as negotiators.

Board members and chief administrators can insist on the protection of management rights at the bargaining table—

not just high-sounding contract clauses but genuine, specific powers. They must also reexamine the internal relationships among their various administrative groups, becoming more sensitive to the views and concerns of the campus administrators who are responsible for implementing the terms of negotiated contracts. But as long as faculty have a role in selecting administrators, developing a management function will be difficult.

Eventually the chief administrator will have to accept the adversary relationship inherent in collective bargaining. To hope for a collegial role as consultant to the faculty, as was reported in a role orientation study of Michigan community college presidents, is unrealistic; if achieved it could lead to the employer negotiator becoming a second executive (Murton, 1974).

In sum, collective bargaining has made great headway in community colleges. As more states pass legislation permitting collective bargaining more colleges will be engaged in the process. Florida, Oregon, and California may be among the most active areas for collective bargaining in the middle 1970s.

Collective bargaining is essentially a thrust by faculty for participation in governance. How much participation they acquire depends upon the skill of their representatives at the bargaining table, the skill of the employer representatives, and the community environment.

Collective bargaining is a process of negotiation between equals: the employee and the employer representatives. The employee-employer relationship contravenes the collegiality principle so long held dear in higher education.

Collective bargaining introduces a change in relationships among administrators. It creates a situation which imperils the security of the second- and third-echelon administrators since they have minimal influence during negotiations.

The composition of the employee unit has been expanding to include not only full-time teaching faculty but part-time faculty, librarians, counselors, laboratory technicians, instructional-resources personnel, chairpersons and nonsupervisory administrators such as registrars.

The employees may be represented by one organization or by two or more organizations through a representative group. The employer unit may be a local board of trustees for one or a number of colleges in a district, a state board acting for all the colleges in a state, a university board of regents acting for all the colleges within the system, the state executive, or a county government or a combination of two or more county governments.

The faculty position is that management is the "servant" of the faculty. Their leaders seem to strive for a governance pattern similar to that of universities.

Collective-bargaining contracts introduce the employee bargaining group as another bureaucratic organization affecting the life of faculty members. The president of the group or a shop steward becomes a quasi-administrative officer acting as the representative of the employees, especially during grievance procedures, and a general watchdog over compliance with the terms of the contract.

We may be heading toward a situation in which administrators become ministerial officers implementing provisions of contracts.

Chapter Three

Free Tuition
Faces Its Doom

A constant campaign for no or low tuition is maintained by many community college educators who rise to defend this policy whenever it is threatened. Their pronouncements attract attention but have little effect on legislators, governors, trustees, and administrators faced with the necessity of balancing budgets. In fact, increasing numbers of colleges are resorting to tuition and fees to help make up the difference between their budget requirements and inadequate state and local revenues. With no reversal of this trend, the most distinguishing characteristic of the community college except for open access will have disappeared or have been drastically modified by the end of the 1970s.

As government funds become difficult to obtain, pressure mounts to have the costs of higher education shared by individuals as well as by society. This pressure comes from economists, businessmen, a small number of community college educators, and groups such as the Committee for Economic Development (*The Management and Financing of Colleges*, 1973) and the New York Task Force on Financing Higher Education (*Higher Education in New York State . . .* , 1973). As Cheit (1973) points out, in coming years efforts to have students pay an increased portion of the cost of postsecondary education will be given higher priority than maintaining high quality or extending access to higher education.

For a time also it seemed as if the Carnegie Commission had reversed its support of low tuition for community colleges. Following a barrage of criticism, however, the Commission announced that its recommendation for increasing tuition to narrow the gap between public and private institutions was not intended to apply to community colleges (The Carnegie Commission on Higher Education, 1973b). Subsequently, in a special report on tuition, the Commission specifically stated that its recommendations for a change in traditional tuition policy "exempted two-year colleges from any suggested increases, favoring low or preferably no tuition for them" (The Carnegie Commission on Higher Education, 1974, p. 4).

The debate on tuition policies indicates little disagreement on the assumptions that an educated citizenry is an asset to society, that economic, social, and psychological benefits accrue to people who have been to college, and that government has an obligation to aid individuals from low-income families. The major difference revolves around the question "How should the costs of higher education be shared by society and individuals?" And this question in turn revolves around others: "Who benefits most from education, society or the individual?" "Why should those (usually from the low-income group) who do not receive a higher education subsidize the more affluent middle- and high-income groups that attend college?" (The Carnegie Commission on Higher Education, 1973a).

Any discussions of who should pay for education must take into consideration the effect of tuition on access. This effect is difficult to determine, but the universal juxtaposition of recommendations for financial aid with proposals for tuition increases adds weight to the general opinion about the negative effect of tuition on access, especially for individuals from low- and middle-income families. Almost every group studying access to higher education reports that costs of tuitions and fees are a major obstacle. This is as true of the findings of the Committee for Economic Development, which supports tuition, as of those of the Carnegie Commission, which does not. From 1972 census data, the National Commission on the Financing of Postsecondary Education concludes that the participation rate of eighteen- to twenty-four-year olds whose family income is ten thousand dollars or more is twice the rate of those from families with an annual income under ten thousand dollars (*Financing Postsecondary Education* . . . , 1973). The close correlation between tuition and enrollment also gives rise to the claim that "for every hundred dollar increase in tuition, there is a 250,000 decrease in college enrollments" (Leslie and Johnson, 1974, p. 28).

Despite the seemingly close relationship between income and access to higher education, some educators doubt that a cause-effect relationship exists or even that income is the most important factor in access. They agree with Richardson (1972), who maintains that the assumption that people will not attend college unless subsidized is no longer valid. Several facts support Richardson's view. An indirect confirmation is the general tendency of disadvantaged students not to attend inexpensive community colleges and technical schools but to enroll instead in high-tuition proprietary schools (Wilms, 1974). Another support for Richardson's position is the high percentage of students—50 percent or more in some colleges—who work part- or full-time to keep themselves in college. Richardson's view is also partially supported by the finding of the National Commission on the Financing of Postsecondary Education that inequities of access are not related to family income alone (*Financing Postsecondary Education* . . . , 1973). The Commission found that the factor with the strongest statistical relationship to college-going is high school curriculum; a student who follows a college-preparatory program has a 70 to 85 percent chance of going to college. The second most important factor is educational attainment of the father; the greater his attainment, the greater the likelihood of his child's enrolling in a postsecondary institution. Leslie (1973) designated geography as the major factor in predicting whether a student goes to college and which institution he selects, an observation that is borne out by community college enrollment patterns—the majority of students live within five to ten miles of the campus and the rate of college-going rises in areas where such colleges are established.

Richardson's view finds additional support in community colleges. The most persuasive argument is that between 1960 and 1970 community college enrollments more than quadrupled, with colleges charging tuition sharing the increase with tuition-free colleges. This growth rate has decreased since the end of the Vietnam War, but in both numbers and percentages the enrollment figures of the 1960s are spectacular and seem to confirm the belief that tuition does not prevent any motivated youngster who wants an education from attending college. Although grants, work study programs, and loans are available, they are not large enough to account for the dramatic enrollment increase. Nationally, about 39 percent of fall 1973 entering freshmen in two-year colleges reported no concern about financing, with 46 percent indicating some concern and 15 percent, major concern (Astin and others, n.d.).

In addition, while the size of tuition may have a major bearing on the enrollment of four-year and university students, it has less effect on community college enrollments. "For almost all ranges of increased tuition, students in public four-year institutions are more responsive to tuition changes than students in public two-year colleges" (*Financing Postsecondary Education . . .* , 1973, p. 312).

The debate over tuition reveals that more than the effects on open access are involved however. Part of Richardson's (1972) objection to the no- or low-tuition policy is based on the danger of "isolating two-year colleges as the free segment of higher education." He feels that the no-tuition policy, if deemed necessary for the public welfare, should be instituted in all colleges. Underlying this objection, rarely set forth with Richardson's candor, is the fear that if the two-year colleges become institutions primarily for the underprivileged and those with the least preparation for higher education, they will in time suffer the deterioration now affecting inner-city high schools.

For some or all of the reasons just outlined, a sizable number of community college administrators and faculty members do not agree with the no-tuition advocates. Collins argues that since "higher education brings dividends to the general society, to the employers in the economy, and to those who secure this higher education, there is good reason for suggesting that these particular groups . . . should be the ones to make the investment that produces the dividends" (1970, p. 1). As do other proponents of tuition, Collins proposes that financial aid and loans be made available to low-income students and that repayment of loans be postponed until the student begins earning a minimum salary after graduation. He also suggests that if students pay tuition they will be more likely to insist on "a say in college policies," not to enroll or continue in "a college with an outmoded or irrelevant curriculum," and not to "tolerate an arrogant, punitive, or incompetent instructor."

Richardson argues that the recommendation "for no tuition or low tuition in community colleges represents an unrealistic approach at a time when resources are extremely limited for all forms of higher education. . . . [If] students should pay a defined part of the costs of their education in public four-year colleges and universities in proportion to their ability to pay, I see no good reason for not initiating similar practices in two-year colleges, provided that the option is there to provide free education to those who cannot afford to pay" (1972, p. 25). These arguments are sometimes echoed in college catalogs; the Dixie College (Utah) 1971–1972 catalog, for example, states that assuming part of the cost of education through payment of tuition and fees is the obligation of every student and his or her parents.

To set the debate in context, let us look at the current status of tuition in community colleges to see how widespread it is and how high it is becoming. Although in regard to the payment of tuition students are classified as resident (or in-district), state nonresident (or out-of-district), and out-of-state nonresident, here we focus on tuition for resident students. No distinction exists between resident and state nonresident in state-supported community colleges. In locally supported colleges, state nonresident students are charged a tuition higher than resident students but lower than out-of-state students. In both cases the number of nonresident students and the amount of income obtained from them are relatively small (Lombardi, 1973).

Educators make a distinction between tuition and fees. Tuition is a charge for instruction, while a fee is a charge for a service only peripherally related to instruction. For certain items classified as fees—such as parking, health care, and athletics—this distinction is valid, but for others—such as graduation, matriculation, models in art classes, music rooms, and laboratory equipment—it is less tenable. A preference for the term *fee* rather than *tuition* reflects educators' unease at the contradiction between the concept of the open door and the practice of charging tuition for instruction. The use of the term *fee* may also be a circumvention of state laws that forbid tuition but permit fees. Arizona, California, and New York City, for example, have "no-tuition" policies that are eroded by various laboratory fees of doubtful legality, parking and health-care fees, and the fees for certain categories of adult students now charged in at least twenty-two districts in California (Gold, 1972). For the student, these recurrent and compulsory fees are difficult to distinguish from tuition. It makes little difference to a student whether a charge of $41.20 per semester in New York City, $45 in Phoenix, or $60 in Prescott, Arizona, is called a fee or tuition.

Methods of reporting and classification complicate estimates of tuition and fees as a percentage of the total budget. For example, for the period 1964–1970, Harrisburg Area Community College received 44.1 percent of its revenue from tuition and fees, yet Pennsylvania law limits tuition to one-third of operating costs (*President's Progress Report,* 1970). A 1970–1971 survey of fifteen states reported tuition income of $88.1 million, which covered 18.9 percent of operating costs and 0.9 percent of capital outlay expenditures (Spencer, 1972a, 1972b). A lower national estimate for covered operating costs, 14.3 percent, was reported by the National Commission on the Financing of Postsecondary Education (*Financing Postsecondary Education* . . . , 1973).

Wattenbarger and others (1973) report that in only four of the forty-two states that had two-year colleges in 1965 did no college charge tuition or fees. In 1970 only two of the forty-nine states that had community colleges reported no colleges charging anything. By 1972, all states had two-year colleges, and in all of them one or more colleges charged tuition or fees; in thirty-three states, every college collected (Connor and others, 1973). The amount of tuition has increased as well. Huther (1971) reports that 18 percent of the colleges charged between two hundred and five hundred dollars per year in 1960, 68 percent in 1968. Since Huther's study, tuition and fees have continued to rise.

The experiences of the locally controlled colleges in Illinois, where tuition is optional, illustrate these trends. Once tuition is adopted by a district, there is no return to a tuition-free policy. Of eight districts that began operations with a no-tuition policy, only one has retained it. About 20 percent of the Illinois districts increase their tuition each year, and since 1969–1970 the number of colleges charging $10 to $17 per credit hour ($300 to $510 per year) has more than tripled.

Sampling 283 public colleges, Peterson (1972) found that in 1971 tuition averaged $214 and that the average rise for 1971 over 1970 was about $18, a 9 percent increase. Some of the colleges included in the sample however did not charge tuition at all. The National Commission on the Financing of Postsecondary Education reported an average of $200 for 1972–1973 (*Financing Postsecondary Education* . . . , 1973, p. 75).

There are few exceptions to this trend toward greater dependence on tuition and fees as sources of revenue. Rarely does a college or state that has initiated tuition revert to a no-tuition policy or reduce tuition. Not including fees, tuition charges of $300 to $400 are becoming common, with some colleges in New York charging $650. By the end of the 1970s, average charges will probably approach $500, with some colleges imposing as much as $1000. In 1971–1972 constant dollars, Lind

(1973) projects student charges of $302 for 1980–1981. These increases may come sooner if education fails to regain its priority position for funds, if the gross national product remains stationary, or if inflation continues at the rate of 10 percent plus.

Although a few states have adopted the same tuition for lower-division students in all segments of higher education, tuition in community colleges will probably be lower than in four-year colleges for two reasons: open access to higher education is interpreted as applying to community colleges rather than to the more selective institutions; and states are trying to control enrollments in senior colleges, which are costly to operate, by encouraging students to enroll in the less costly community colleges through lower tuition.

Until now, although governors and legislators look on tuition in all state colleges as an important source of revenue, they have been reluctant to shift more than one-third of the cost of instruction to the students, preferring instead to increase state aid to the colleges. But the outlook for the continuance of this pattern is not propitious. As inflation continues, as faculty gain salary increases, and as other demands are made on state funds, tuition will probably rise at a steeper yearly rate than the recent 8 to 10 percent. The situation in Maryland is typical: in fifteen of the sixteen colleges there costs per student in 1972 exceeded fourteen hundred dollars, which meant that tuition had to be increased since state appropriations are limited to half the costs of instruction and cannot exceed seven hundred dollars (*Master Plan for Community Colleges* . . . , 1973). Equally unpropitious are the recommendations made by influential groups such as the Committee for Economic Development and the New York Task Force on Financing Higher Education for an increase in tuition up to half of the full cost of instruction and for narrowing the tuition gap between public and private colleges and universities.

Thus, because tuition and fees are needed to supplement state appropriations and property tax receipts, they will persist at increased rates in the community colleges. However reluctantly, administrators, faculty members, and leaders of professional organizations who have a large stake in the maintenance of the enterprise will find reasons for justifying the charges. Like decision makers in other public enterprises, they will not choose to make economies that would result in contraction of programs and personnel, even though such a course might be an alternative to higher tuition and fees. Their addition of functions and services in the face of decreased enrollment growth will increase costs and add to the pressure to require students to pay for their education.

The rapid growth in federal and state appropriations for student aid—four billion dollars in federal appropriations and four hundred million dollars in state appropriations (*Financing Postsecondary Education* . . . , 1973)—makes it easy to justify tuition since it is assumed that student aid is readily available for all who need it. But, even though the rate of increase in these appropriations is higher than the rate of increase in full-time enrollment and tuition, student aid—federal and state combined—is still inadequate for many high school graduates.

For those who believe that any tuition is an obstacle to universal access, all financial-aid packages seem to beg the question. Carol Van Alstyne (1974), chief economist for the American Council on Education, sees no inherent reason why the financing of public postsecondary education should differ essentially from the financing of elementary or secondary education, a view that goes back to the proposals of the President's Commission on Higher Education (1947) and the Educational Policies Commission (*Report of the Educational Policies Commission,* 1964). A no-tuition policy would eliminate the means test so widely applied in the distribution of student aid. It would also prevent a confrontation with middle-income parents who feel that their children are losers in the distribution of financial aid, most of which is given to students from low-income families.

However, both proponents and opponents of tuition agree that financial aid is a necessity if all individuals are to have open access to, or equal opportunity for, a postsecondary education. The major difference between the two sides is that opponents of tuition do not consider financial aid to be a substitute for no or low tuition. To them experience with financial aid does not warrant optimism that enough will be available for all who need it. They suspect that if the low-tuition policy is scrapped, college education will again be available only to a financially privileged few ("Meany Urges Labor Federations . . . ," 1973). Yet by lobbying for more student aid, the no-tuition advocates indirectly contribute to the tuition proponents' argument that such aid ensures no individual's being deprived of the opportunity to attend college.

The increasing imposition of tuition in community colleges indicates that they are no longer open to all those who wish to attend, with the only major requirement for admission a high school diploma or the equivalent. A more accurate statement would add "all those able to pay the necessary tuition and fees," often a substantial amount for many potential students. Community college educators' efforts to soften the impact of tuition and fees by calling them modest, by comparing them with the much higher charges of four-year colleges and universities, or by offering scholarships and loans cannot obscure the fact that the open-door policy has been modified drastically.

If community college educators would reverse the trend toward higher tuition they must give up their acquiescence to the low-tuition policy and adopt the position articulated by Van Alstyne—that the financing of public postsecondary education should resemble that of the lower schools. Such a switch would at least make their position on tuition consistent with their dedication to the open door.

Chapter Four

Affirmative Action Arises

Certain social issues have a way of reemerging periodically in different configurations, often in direct response to organized pressure. Proportional representation for economic, ethnic, religious, and political groups is one of them, and American history is filled with attempts by one group or another to achieve parity in employment, political office, housing, and schooling. Yet all these issues are interrelated, and discrimination in any area for or against any group impinges on all other groups.

Today, members of ethnic minorities and women are the focus of recruitment and hiring policies. Since both groups have suffered from discrimination in American colleges and universities, federal legislation is making it both legally and morally imperative that employment policies in higher education afford equal opportunities for all who are qualified. Under Executive Order 11246, institutions holding federal contracts must be able to demonstrate that no discrimination exists in any aspect of employment and, further, that affirmative action is being taken to remedy the effects of past discrimination. The burden of proof is thus placed on the administration of a college or university to provide evidence of its innocence rather than on the employee or federal government to prove the administration's guilt.

As a result of this law, reports can be found that both reveal discriminatory practices and pose directions for alleviating them. Most major universities have indicated their position on various practices, as demonstrated by a host of documents in the Educational Resources Information Center (ERIC) collection. But of the 119 documents on affirmative action found in the ERIC system in spring 1974, only five were concerned specifically with community colleges.

This lack of available documentation does not mean that affirmative action has missed these institutions, however. Many community colleges employ affirmative action officers or faculty members to help both the institution and individuals affected by discriminatory practices. And pressure groups—student, professional, and community—have encouraged the colleges to increase the proportion of minorities and women that they employ. In addition, affirmative action in other postsecondary institutions is certain to affect the community colleges.

The policy is not without opposition, however, with contradictory positions sometimes heatedly advocated. On one side are those who believe in a meritocracy, who say that valuable and increasingly scarce positions should not be given to people who happen to be female or members of ethnic minorities if they are less qualified than their male or majority-group counterparts. On the other side are those who feel that social justice has not been achieved unless all groups are represented equally in all walks of life. Nevertheless, before long affirmative action will certainly be universally pursued—at least overtly.

The term *affirmative action* may be new but the concept is hardly unique. History provides a background of protests— medieval serfs against landowners, American slaves against masters, groups against public laws that barred them from schools, jobs, or housing.

The Civil Rights movement of the 1960s gave rise to a new form of action—one into which the federal government stepped with a thud. While the process is not firmly cemented, the policy is established. The United States government withholds funds from those schools and colleges that continue to make personnel selections that exclude minority groups or women. And although there is often more lip service given to the idea of affirmative action than there is actual implementation, few people or institutions openly defy the mandate.

Some basis for the government's policy is seen in the historical view of women as reflected by Koontz (1972), who notes that while women's contributions to American educational leadership have been important from colonial times to the present, they have often been ignored. Women have suffered from prevailing negative attitudes ranging from masculine fears of economic competition to the age-old theories regarding their mental, physical, and emotional competencies. It is now time, he asserts, for education to dispel sexism and to train people for economic, political, and social equality.

Corroborating Koontz's stance, Manicur (1969) argues that women traditionally have had to assume an aggressive role in order to become educated. Indeed, records dating as far back as the seventeenth and eighteenth centuries point to their difficulties in finding opportunities to study and learn. Superficially, it may appear that women willingly accepted this subservient role, but one need only study the culture and attitudes of the time to understand the manifold barriers they had to overcome to be permitted even minimum educational experiences.

The American Association of University Women (AAUW) demands that colleges and universities remedy existing inequities in higher education that deprive women of quality education, educational opportunity, and leadership (*Standards for Women in Higher Education* . . . , n.d.). To this end, the report states, every institution must develop an affirmative action policy and action plan for students, faculty, administrators, nonacademic staff, and trustees. Further, a statement of the policy, including a plan and timetable for implementation, should be published and available for review by any person in the institution. These AAUW standards are stated in terms of general objectives for women students, faculty members, and administrators, and for administrative practice. They also suggest related operational criteria for assessing the achievement of those objectives. Such recommendations reinforce traditional national goals. Institutions of higher learning have been regarded historically as the standard bearers of high moral, ethical, and democratic conduct. Yet, until federal intervention became necessary to mitigate discriminatory practices, in both admissions and employment procedures, they ignored their obligations.

Affirmative action rests on five bodies of law: federal laws, Executive Order 11246, institutional guidelines, judicial decisions, and state laws. A number of issues are covered by the guidelines issued by the Department of Health, Education, and Welfare Office for Civil Rights on how colleges and universities should work to eliminate discrimination against women and minorities. For example, they denote specific legal provisions to ensure that in performing a government contract in excess of ten thousand dollars the contractor will not discriminate against any employees or applicants. Nondiscrimination requires the elimination of existing discriminatory conditions and mandates that the employer make additional efforts to "recruit, employ, and promote" qualified members of groups formerly excluded (Lester, 1974).

The Executive Order requires that contractors not discriminate against any employee or applicant for employment and that they take affirmative action to ensure that applicants are employed and treated during their employment without regard to race, color, religion, sex, or national origin. A conclusion of noncompliance is not required if the original goals in employment are not met because qualified minorities and women are unavailable, because the number of openings is inaccurately estimated, or because of changed employment market conditions. However, if the cause of failure to comply with the Executive Order is inattention to the nondiscrimination and affirmative action policies, then the contractor may be found out of compliance with the law. Not only must an employer establish in detail its standards and procedures governing employment, it must also make explicit its commitment to equal employment opportunities by recruiting women and minority persons as actively as it recruits nonminority males.

Despite the fact that the Executive Order covers both women and members of minority groups, a number of people view it primarily in terms of women. The National Organization for Women (NOW) takes the position that while universities were quick to respond to discrimination against black academicians in the 1960s, they have often ignored cries from women: "In 1970, the Women's Equity Action League and the National Organization for Women filed a class action suit against more than two hundred colleges and universities, charging sex discrimination in hiring, promotion, salary, tenure, and other conditions of employment. . . . [Although] the language in all guidelines forbids discrimination for many causes, it should be quite clear that the current controversy stems almost exclusively from discrimination on the basis of sex. Were only racial minorities involved, it is hard to imagine a similar furor" (*Goals vs. Quotas* . . . , 1972, p. 1).

NOW documents the position of women in universities as the last hired, usually at lower levels than similarly qualified men, receiving less pay, holding fewer desirable teaching assignments, and receiving fewer promotions. "Nepotism rules mitigate against them, childbearing is regarded as just grounds for exclusion, and harassment by misogynist colleagues is all too often tolerated. The truism that a woman has to be twice as good to get half as far is still evidenced by the experience of academic women" (*Goals vs. Quotas* . . . , 1972, p. 1). In current practice the Civil Rights issues mandating equality for minority elements of society are being interpreted for women.

The laws governing affirmative action programs and sex discrimination on campus are examined by Shulman (1972), who describes the approaches universities and colleges have taken to comply with the law. Several steps are designated, including advertising new positions in journals that reach minorities and women; providing training to upgrade employees; assuring representation of women and minorities on search committees; establishing adequate employee grievance mechanisms; making provision for adequate day care for employees' children; initiating sensible and fair policies for maternity, child-rearing, and other types of leave; equalizing retirement plans and other fringe benefits; liberalizing policies on part-time employment, including tenure appointments; and requiring that proposals for hiring a candidate who is not a member of a protected class be accompanied by a statement that women and minority candidates were actively sought before a decision was made.

Institutions find it easier to adopt affirmative action for women than for minorities because questions of qualification are often reduced. Historically, ethnic minorities may have been inadequately educated, but numerous women have received graduate degrees and are often better prepared for jobs than their male counterparts. Thus, bringing women into the work force does not imply the "lowering of standards" that so many fear, and it is a comparatively easy way of meeting the federal law requirements while simultaneously protecting institutional "quality."

Colleges and universities are trying in various ways to comply with the Executive Order. One problem is identifying the specific effects of previous discriminatory practices. Most colleges have three general categories of administrator: those who maintain the physical plant, manage the business, and develop alumni and public relations; those who work in admissions, student affairs, counseling, and student aid; and those academic leaders, such as presidents, chancellors, provosts, and deans. Mattfield (1972) notes that in Ivy League schools the first two categories have an equal distribution between the sexes while the third is slanted toward males. At Harvard, for example, the appointments of women are concentrated at the lower levels of administrative employees.

Similar conditions prevail for faculty. At Brooklyn College, for example, female professors may equal males at the assistant or associate levels, but they seem unable to break through to full professorships. At the University of Chicago few women are hired in social science faculties, and few of these remain for more than one appointment (three years). The first appointment for women is usually as instructor or lecturer rather than assistant professor, and those who eventually become full professors do so by rising through the "women's departments" or by being brought in from other universities at a tenured position (Freeman, 1969). White and White (1973) present data on the status of women in full-time teaching positions in 164 college and university art departments, a status that can best be summarized by the relationship, "The higher, the fewer." Further, in those departments that have PhDs on their faculties, the percentage of women with doctorates exceeds the percentage of men by almost 25 percent. Hence, although women are concentrated at the lower ranks, on the average they are more highly trained than their male colleagues.

Studies at the University of Kansas offer no substantive proof of overt academic discrimination against women or of fewer National Defense student loans being given to women, a finding contrary to one at Michigan State University (*A Compilation of Data . . .* , 1970) where more women than men were accepted to graduate study but fewer received financial aid. Just what proportion of males to females try for fellowships is another question. In 1972, Fields reported that relatively few women do.

The recommendations that emerge from studies of policies are similar to those formulated from a survey at Indiana State University (*The Status of Faculty Women . . .* , 1972). It was recommended that Indiana State reassert its support of the Civil Rights Act by requiring departments or schools with few or no women to examine the national degree lists and seek qualified women; by having the administration conduct periodic checks to see in what department women retain their rank longer than men; and by taking immediate steps to remedy salary differences.

Representative of other recommendations are those emanating from the University of Minnesota. Formulas for departmental hiring and procedures are presented in a report on equal opportunities, and general principles are indicated to ensure fair treatment in tenure and promotion; to uniformly apply, collect, and disseminate information; to specify criteria; and to equalize salaries (*Report of Subcommittee . . .* , 1971).

Also recommended are female appointments to key administrative positions and provisions for developmental opportunities.

Considerable resistance has been engendered by the academic community to the Department of Health, Education, and Welfare's Executive Order. The controversy focuses on just what the government does and does not require. Some academicians have interpreted goals and timetables as rigid quotas based on characteristics other than merit, and they view them as undemocratic, antilibertarian, and a short route to destroying academic freedom.

The guidelines for affirmative action do, however, establish procedures for grievance that have become a recourse for a number of people (Irving, 1972). From 1970 to 1972, in fact, formal charges of sex discrimination were filed against 360 colleges and universities, and in 1972 a national conference was held at the University of Michigan to address legal problems of employing women in universities. Indeed, increasing numbers of women are testing the courts' powers to redress their grievances (Fields, 1973). Although few suits had gone through the courts at the time, Fields reports that "some women's rights advocates predict that litigation will play an increasingly important part in the campaign for equal treatment of women in academic admissions and employment. . . . Progress is likely to be slow, however, . . . because many judges are loath to enter the academic sphere" (p. 3). Some cases brought to court since 1973 involve the payment of lower retirement benefits to women and the denial of tenure or promotion by such institutions as Pace College in New York, the Teachers Insurance and Annuity Association, Texas Technological University, University of California at Berkeley, and Florida State University.

The first injunction ever granted to an academic woman charging her institution with sex discrimination was issued in 1973 by a United States District Court in Pittsburgh (*Johnson v. University of Pittsburgh*). The University Medical School of Pittsburgh was enjoined from terminating the employment of an assistant professor of biochemistry by denying her tenure. Issues included back pay, reinstallment with tenure, space allo-

cation, and harassment or interference with the plaintiff's research.

Some people question the Executive Order in terms of
reverse discrimination. Writing for the Anti-Defamation League
of B'nai B'rith, Epstein (1973) observes that equal opportunity, justice, and fair treatment remain the goals of the League
—for Jews and for all other Americans. But, because the criterion of an individual is of prime importance, they react to the
growing calls for preferential treatment and racial quotas,
which they view as discrimination in reverse. One finds many
examples of the concept of affirmative action programs to end
discrimination being turned into programs of racial quotas or
preferential treatment. "The only morally justifiable answer is
that those institutions responsible for past acts of discrimination should make the sacrifices. The fundamental wrong in
preferential treatment is that individuals who have no responsibility for past discrimination are forced to sacrifice their opportunities to pay the debt that society owes to those previously
discriminated against."

But Task Force for NOW defends the Order (*Goals vs.
Quotas* . . . , 1972, pp. 2–4):

> If universities were in fact required to hire X number
> of women, blacks, or other minorities solely on the basis of
> their membership in a particular group, this would indeed
> be reprehensible. Quotas have, as often noted, been used
> to *limit* the participation of various minorities. They are
> maximums which deny opportunities to qualified persons
> because of birth [while existing systems for academic hiring
> already rely on a quota restricting the employment of women
> and minorities]. The goals required by Executive Order
> 11246 do not do this; they open doors to those who have
> unfairly been excluded in the past. . . . We support the
> government's efforts [and take the] position that such enforce-
> ment will widen civil liberties rather than restricting them.

The issue of reverse discrimination reached the United
States Supreme Court in spring 1974, when Marco De Funis,
a white male, asserted that lesser qualified applicants who were

members of minority groups had been admitted to the University of Washington law school while he had been rejected (*De Funis et al. v. Odegaard*). The university was in effect using preferential admission policies to increase the number of minority-group students they accepted for enrollment. The question to be decided by the court was whether preferential admissions for certain groups would lead to quotas rather than to attainment of admissions and hiring goals as set forth in the Civil Rights Act. However, after De Funis' case was filed, he was admitted to law school under a lower court order and was graduated in 1974, thus allowing the Supreme Court to avoid a decision.

The De Funis case reflects a substantial backlash against the federal affirmative action program, and resistance to the Executive Order persists. For example, some thirty-five "illustrative complaints" were submitted to federal officials by six national Jewish organizations, including the Anti-Defamation League of B'nai B'rith, The American Jewish Committee, and the American Jewish Congress, supporting their contention that preferential treatment is widespread. And a nationwide committee, which includes such people as Bruno Bettelheim, Nathan Glazer, Sidney Hook, Seymour Martin Lipset, Eugene Rostow, and Paul Seabury, has filed complaints with the United States Office for Civil Rights.

While these critics of the affirmative action program acknowledge that women and minorities have been discriminated against and that efforts are needed to increase their representation on college faculties, they argue that the "affirmative-action program—through its insistence that universities set 'numerical goals' and 'timetables' for hiring—is forcing institutions to abandon 'merit hiring,' penalizing well-qualified white males, debasing educational standards, and threatening institutional autonomy" (Van Dyne, 1973b, p. 4). Whether time and experience will resolve some of these protests, as well as alleviate discrimination, is yet to be seen.

Chait and Ford (1973) postulate that the most significant ramification of affirmative action may be yet to come; that compliance with these regulations will either end or transform academe's most established and distinctive personnel practice—tenure.

Because increased hiring of women and minorities depends largely on openings and since openings are diminished by tenure, tenure becomes a block to affirmative action. By limiting the criteria colleges and universities may use in hiring and retaining faculty, the courts undercut the basis of tenure and may eventually eliminate it.

Affirmative action policies prohibit the use of those evaluative criteria not related to job performance that perpetuate discrimination. Such criteria are clarified in Petrillo's (1971, p. 1) summary of the decision in *Griggs v. Duke Power Company* (401 U.S. 424 [1971]). "The requirement of either a high school diploma or success in a standardized general education test as a prior condition to employment is prohibited by the Civil Rights Act of 1964, Title VII (1) where the employer cannot establish that either standard significantly relates to competence in the job at issue; (2) where such standards have the effect of disqualifying a significantly higher proportion of blacks than whites (that is, if the effect is discriminatory even where there is no intention to discriminate); and (3) where formerly the jobs were limited to whites under a prior policy of discrimination practiced by the employer."

While the *Griggs* case has only indirect implications for tenure and other academic practices, the *Armstead v. Starkville Municipal School District* (325 F. Suppl. 560) decision is directly connected. It states that by tying teachers' appointments and retention to attaining a master's degree and a specified score on Graduate Record Examinations, a public school board unlawfully discriminates against blacks.

Discrimination in academe, as Astin and Bayer (1972) note, does not begin for a woman when she accepts an appointment at a college or university. Rather it is rooted in early childhood socialization for "appropriate" sex role behavior and attitudes; differential treatment and expectations of girls and boys by their parents, teachers, and peers throughout early childhood and adolescence; and differential opportunities for admission to undergraduate and graduate school. When women enter teaching careers in colleges and universities they have interests, aspirations, expectations, educational backgrounds, and experiences that differ from those of their male counterparts.

Pifer (1971) reiterates the point that in both the attainment of degrees and in subsequent employment, women have been discriminated against in higher education, and that compared with their male counterparts they are underemployed and underpaid. Women who have the ability and desire for careers in education and the professions should be given a fair chance to have them. And that fair chance, because of the accumulated negative impact of our cultural heritage, must include active encouragement and assistance to women.

Active encouragement, if it is sincere and is to prove effective, requires basic changes in attitude, and most women in the academic world have found that these changes come about after behavioral changes have taken place. Thus, they have been pushing for revisions to end nepotism policies, establish appropriate grievance procedures, revise tenure rules to include part-time work, develop women's studies programs, maintain child-care centers, analyze fringe benefits, establish fair maternity leave policies, prorate part-time work at a rate commensurate with full-time work, provide open admissions for women in coeducational institutions, abolish student rules for one sex, and encourage women to return to school. Now that these changes are being implemented—primarily through the withholding of federal funds from institutions participating in discriminatory practices—it is hoped that related attitudinal changes will also become a reality. Such a result would benefit the world of work in general as well as education itself—from kindergarten to graduate school.

While the movement for women's equality is by no means new in the United States, the changing life patterns of women in the work world, the recent legal basis for equal opportunity, and the modification of sex roles and aspirations due to reduction of bias in elementary and secondary schools are causing important changes (Raffel, 1973). Such changes are reflected in higher education, although, some would say, not quickly enough. Particularly beneficial to women are such features as flexible course hours, part-time and short-term courses, group and individual counseling, financial aid for part-time study, flexible residence requirements, removal of age restrictions, liberal transfer of course credits, curriculum geared to adult experiences, credit by examination, refresher courses, reorientation courses, child-care facilities, relaxation of time requirements for degrees, job placement, and assistance for nontraditional professions. Some of these features are incorporated into most colleges and universities but they must be expanded. Change is often a threatening and sometimes a painful process, but the modification caused by the women's movement will be advantageous to women, men, and higher education as a whole if it is approached in a constructive manner.

In addition to the problems of tenure institutions must deal with nepotism. At Tufts, for example, there has been considerable concern about the university position regarding this issue. Dunkle and Simmons (1972) advocate the employment of qualified academics who are married couples, noting that antinepotism policies, originally passed to protect colleges and universities from the political pressures of having to hire incompetent people with influential connections and to prevent the formation of father-son alliances, are now used almost exclusively as rationalizations for not hiring or promoting women who are married to faculty members. The elimination of antinepotism practices would have the following effects (according to the Tufts researchers): (1) undergraduates would be able to see husbands and wives working together professionally and dealing with the problems of dual-career marriages; (2) undergraduate women would be exposed to more academic career models; (3) qualified women and men married to faculty members would be better able to utilize their talents and resources; (4) Tufts would be assuming a position of leadership in providing equal opportunity for women; and (5) the university would have a larger pool of qualified female academics from which to choose.

Looking at variations of this policy, Simon and Clark (1966) studied the relative productivity of women with doctorates by comparing teaching and research contributions of recent PhDs in four categories: (1) married women whose husbands are employed at universities with nepotism rules, (2) married women whose husbands are not on university faculties or are employed at universities without nepotism rules, (3) unmarried women, and (4) men. It was found that teaching duties occupy the time of most respondents; unmarried women are as likely to hold associate or full professorships as men; and men earn more than women, and unmarried women earn more than married women. The mean number of articles published by women who claim to be affected by antinepotism rules is higher than that for other women and for men. Nevertheless, 15 percent of the married women responding to the survey believe that their careers have been hurt by antinepotism regulations.

Related to this report is the proposal of the Carnegie Commission on Higher Education that there be no antinepotism rules, but that a husband or wife should not be involved in a decision relating to his or her spouse.

Compliance with affirmative action may also lead in the next few years to a conflict between associations that represent white women and those that speak for members of minority groups. Kenneth Tollett, distinguished professor of higher education at Howard University, notes that "the groundswell interest in discrimination against women in higher education is deflecting attention and effort away from steps to correct the more virulent form of discrimination—that against blacks, Chicanos, and Indians." He goes on to say that "minority groups, particularly blacks, deserve better than hostility or aggressive competition from other segments of society—especially indefatigably persistent and outraged middle-class white women (quoted in Watkins, 1973a).

While others argue against this point, saying that the competition between white women and minority-group members is more perception than reality, the Carnegie Commission on Higher Education (1969) reports that in 1969 only 7.3 percent of graduate students were members of minority groups. Today this disproportion works to the advantage of qualified minority candidates—on the job market and in graduate school.

But the Commission finds administrators on campus who

insist on defining the problems of women as distinct from those of minorities, and, should action be taken on this attitude, the present hypothesis of a conflict between women and minorities may become a reality.

The many problems in implementing affirmative action testify to its need. Affirmative action on college campuses will be effective when attitudes change, and then it will no longer be needed.

In sum, few people today would argue against the Executive Order, which has as its goal the elimination of discriminatory practices in higher education. At the same time a careful survey of the literature may well leave one with the feeling that much of what is being done to answer the charge from the outside is simply window-dressing.

Schools affirm their dedication to the mandate, good educational-opportunity officers try to implement the law, and many are genuinely concerned with fair treatment for all and expanded opportunities for those who have been poorly treated in the past. At the same time, many documents reveal superficial attempts to comply with the law. A sense of commitment is often missing. Departments cannot overtly refuse to hire women or other minority-group candidates, but they can say in their seemingly sincere way that they "won't hire their own graduates" (even when graduates are already in residence), that the woman in question is "too old," too experienced for the position, and so forth. When one does not want to do something, it is easy to find ways of preventing it from being done. Call it hedging or defensiveness or fooling oneself, the effect remains: women and minority-group members will not find their places in academe until basic attitudes and perceptions change. One needs to look at the person as an individual, at his or her own strengths and weaknesses, rather than as a member of a particular group or gender. Until we reach that stage, no number of executive orders or referendums will have the effects they must have to ensure a more democratic and more humane society.

Chapter Five

Reduction In Force
and the Seniority System

Triggered by recent massive shifts in enrollment patterns a new acronym has joined the long list of educational jargon: RIF. Reduction in force is well known in other branches of public employment, and those educators who remember the wholesale reductions in the two years before Pearl Harbor when college enrollments fell precipitously are aware of it too. But prior to 1945 administrators and governing boards had little difficulty in dismissing faculty. Many colleges did not grant tenure, hiring instructors instead on yearly contracts. Where tenure laws existed they provided only modest job protection for instructors since they had many loopholes. Colleges with low enrollments were exempt, and probationary instructors could be dismissed at the end of the probationary period without cause and with no recourse to due process. Substitute instructors had no security even though they may have been hired for a semester or a year. Under these conditions administrators had a free hand whether the cause for dismissal was incompetency, insufficient enrollment, or financial difficulty. In sum, reduction in force was a relatively simple process.

During the 1960s RIF was forgotten as enrollments soared and faculty recruitment became frenzied. Few thought about the possibility of a large-scale reduction in force when energies were directed toward seeking candidates for positions in the thirty to fifty new colleges organized each year, replacing faculty pirated by other colleges, and filling new positions to take care of increased enrollment in existing colleges. To make jobs more attractive in this sellers' market, states and colleges began to strengthen job security through tenure laws and regulations. In time the pendulum swung so far in this direction that removing an instructor became a difficult process. Actually, dismissal regulations or laws were invoked infrequently, and then primarily to remove a patently inefficient teacher, a physically or mentally incompetent instructor, a technical or vocational instructor whose skill had become obsolete, or an instructor accused of moral turpitude or serious crime.

Beginning in the early 1970s the situation changed dramatically. The enrollment growth rate slowed, and, at the same time, colleges encountered considerable taxpayer resistance to increased appropriations. As a result a different set of dismissal procedures had to be developed. In many states, however, the laws are still not adequate when large numbers of instructors must be dismissed regardless of their competence.

RIF refers primarily to policies and procedures used when dismissal of tenured and probationary instructors is made necessary by the change in size or nature of the student population, inadequate finances, discontinuance of an area of instruction, or consolidation of districts. This definition differentiates RIF from staff reductions that can be made by cutting back on substitutes and other temporary instructors and by not filling positions vacated by leaves, retirements, and deaths.

Finances are almost always involved in RIF, since in most colleges income is directly related to the number of full-time student equivalents (FTSE) enrolled. Some of the most serious problems occur not because of declining enrollment but because of faulty student projections, and the problem is compounded when projections for an increase in enrollment are followed by an actual decline. On the other hand, under RIF regulations large-scale reductions can take place even though the financial condition and overall enrollment are satisfactory.

RIF has involved fewer community colleges than four-year institutions, but this does not make it any more comfortable for the colleges affected. In spring 1974, nearly every issue of the *Chronicle of Higher Education* told of faculty firing at one campus or another. A 1974 study of 163 colleges reports that, for the three-year period 1971–1973, staff reductions took place or were contemplated in 74 percent of the private four-year institutions, 66 percent of the public four-year institutions, and 41 percent of the two-year colleges (Sprenger and Schultz, 1974). The most serious period for community colleges occurred in fall 1971 when enrollment failed to come up to expectations. This was particularly true in California, Illinois, and Michigan, where colleges had been projecting large enrollment increases every year. Colleges in several other states also reported declines or lower-than-predicted enrollments. Since 1971 the situation has stabilized, and, except for an occasional large-scale reduction such as occurred at Miami-Dade Community College (Florida) in 1972 and lesser occurrences in some Washington State colleges, the community colleges are not suffering to the same extent as the senior institutions, especially state colleges.

The fear that RIF might overtake them has caused shock waves among the staff in innumerable colleges. They know that for the next several years enrollments are more likely to decline than to increase. Although head-count enrollments in 1973 continued to show an annual increase of almost 10 percent, approximately 25 percent of the colleges reported a decline. If FTSE were used, the result would be an even larger number of colleges with declines, since for the past several years the ratio of part-time students has increased markedly. Accordingly, attention is being given to RIF and AAUP statements and to collective bargaining agreements. Numerous conferences on staff reduction policies and practices and on articles concerning the importance of better enrollment projections also attest to growing concern in this unpleasant and troublesome activity.

That more community colleges have not been seriously

inconvenienced by financial difficulty or enrollment decline is attributable to increased financing, better projection techniques, and normal staff attrition due to statutory and early retirements, deaths, leaves, and job changes. An important cushion for many colleges is the part-time staff, mostly instructors in the evening program but also a considerable number in the day program, who have few, if any, rights to their jobs. When enrollment declines they are just not rehired or, if assigned, are dropped. Even tenured instructors have few, if any, rights to their evening or part-time overload assignments if these assignments supplement those of other tenured instructors. Another cushion is conservative staffing—underestimating the number of instructors needed. If enrollments warrant additional instructors it is not difficult in the present buyer's market to recruit competent instructors. With the advent of low-rate enrollment increases administrators are more careful in adding new courses and more prone to eliminate courses that fail to attract students. The most effective method for obviating RIF has been to maintain or increase enrollment more by relaxing admission deadlines, scheduling classes all day and on Saturdays, establishing off-campus centers, advertising in the local press, and distributing flyers and schedules throughout the district. When the enrollment dip is severe the strategies mentioned above help only to the extent that fewer regular instructors are dismissed. For example, at Miami-Dade, some of these strategies helped reduce the number to be dismissed from eighty-four to fifty-eight.

The experiences of colleges such as Miami-Dade, along with court decisions, point up the importance of carefully prepared policies for RIF implementation when it becomes necessary. And implementing procedures are as important as policies —one sets the general guidelines, the other the method of operation. The policies protect the instructor from dismissal, reduction in rank or compensation, and deprivation of any professional advantage for arbitrary or discriminatory reasons; the procedures guarantee that the instructor is "given notice of charges against him, a fair hearing, and related procedural safeguards" (Chanin, 1970). The experience in California (and elsewhere) indicates that cases "to test the sufficiency of dismissal . . . are made on the procedures followed and not on the substance of the allegations" (Briggs, 1972).

Considerable variations exist among RIF policies. They may be no longer than a sentence announcing that "the release of unit members owing to budgetary considerations, decreased enrollments, or requirements for specific technical specialties shall be made on the basis of seniority and qualifications to teach available courses," as at the Community College of Baltimore (Maryland), or they may consist of three or four pages, as at Grays Harbor College (Washington), detailing the various steps in the process from placing responsibility on the person who determines when to apply the rules, to defining the rights of dismissed instructors, and specifying reappointment to jobs and severance pay.

Sometimes a coordinated policy does not exist, yet the college may have a good RIF policy based on state law, college policy and practice, or collective bargaining agreement. The absence of a coordinated policy may be due to the reluctance of one party or the other, usually the employer, to agree to a restatement of existing law and policy on the subject lest the employer be forced to grant greater concessions during the bargaining. An RIF policy proposed by the Hawaii Federation of College Teachers in 1974 was not accepted by the employers, since it would have substituted a seniority system for the merit principle in dismissals. The trend, however, is to incorporate into one document an integrated policy dealing exclusively with RIF.

Although in some states the laws define the conditions for the dismissal of instructors, and in all states responsibility for developing guidelines rests with the college governing board and administration, faculty participation in the RIF process is taken for granted in many colleges and is mandated in a large number. Faculty participation may be a concomitant of collegiality, required by the terms of a collective bargaining contract, the result of legal advice from the state board, or the result of legal advice from the attorney general's office that not only are policies and guidelines imperative but faculty participation is essential to ensure their acceptance of the process, to meet due process requirements, and to reduce litigation.

Faculty participation is greatest in colleges operating under collective bargaining contracts, but occasionally one comes across a contract in which faculty participation does not seem to exist. In the Schenectady County Community College contract under "Termination of Contract" appears the terse statement: "The services of any staff member may be terminated in the event of financial or program retrenchment. The President shall give due consideration to the question of seniority in making his recommendations to the Board of Trustees for their action. There shall be no right of appeal from such action by the Board of Trustees." Paradoxically, where specific guidelines or criteria are established, faculty participation tends to be minimal except to monitor the almost self-administering process. In its memorandum on dismissal of instructors the Los Angeles County Counsel did not include any comments or suggestions for faculty participation.

When it exists, at Grays Harbor, for example, faculty participation may involve nothing more than the opportunity of faculty representatives "to meet with the president who shall fully document the need for . . . reductions in staff . . . and present and explain the major criteria to be used to identify those to be laid off" and, if necessary to eliminate courses, to "identify those courses and explain why they have been judged not to be the most necessary course offerings to maintain the best possible quality educational opportunities." Presumably, the faculty representative would be permitted to offer suggestions, but nothing is written about this in the procedure.

In contrast are statements in many collective bargaining agreements specifying that when there is an impending reduction in force within the bargaining unit the employer shall inform the union in a timely manner and shall obtain the advice and consent of the union before any reduction in force can take place. The Macomb County Community College (Michigan) contract states that the president of the faculty organization "must be given prior notice of and an opportunity to discuss layoffs through the service committee before they are implemented." Agreements also provide that the determination of programs to be maintained or eliminated is to be made by the board of trustees "in consultation with the President, his staff and the Association." At Miami-Dade, which was not operating under a collective bargaining agreement at the time reduction in force became necessary, a broad-based committee of district and campus administrators, department and division chairmen, and representatives from each of the campus senates was organized to develop criteria to be used in the staff reduction program for the 1973–1974 year.

All RIF policies state that dismissals of instructors may take place when enrollment declines, but few indicate how much decline must take place to activate the process or how many instructors may be dismissed. The tendency in some policies is to give major responsibility to the president, who may be required to notify or consult with the recognized employee organization both on the need for a reduction and on the number to be cut. At such consultations the employee representatives may question the president's reasons for the proposed reductions and the number of academic employees he is considering laying off.

Specific criteria are incorporated in some state laws or college policies. Staff reduction may be implemented at Schoolcraft College (Michigan) in the "second consecutive semester in which every member of a given discipline did not have a basic load . . . or whenever any member of a given discipline cannot be assigned any part of a load." California law specifies that "whenever in any school year the average daily attendance (FTSE) . . . for the first six months in which school is in session shall have declined below the corresponding period of *either* of the previous two school years . . . the governing board may terminate the services of not more than a corresponding percentage of the certificated employees of the [college] district, permanent as well as probationary" (*California Education Code,* 1971, Section 13447).

Similarly, in the Fulton-Montgomery Community College (New York) contract, tenured faculty may not be terminated "unless there is an accumulated reduction in Full

Time Equivalent students (total semester hours credit for an academic year, day, evening, winter term, and summer divided by 30) of 10 percent or more below the base figure, 971 Full Time Equivalent students." A cut-off point may be the minimum student-faculty ratio; in New York State, allocations depend on the maintenance of an 18:1 ratio.

When insufficient finances is the reason for dismissals the situation may be more complex. Differences of opinion between the administration and faculty over allocation of funds, along with faculty suspicion that a budget imbalance may be contrived, occur in normal times; they are intensified when a reduction in force is likely to take place. In the RIF policies or laws there are no criteria for financial insufficiency similar to those for enrollment declines.

Whenever a particular kind of service is to be reduced or discontinued an objective criterion is declining enrollment, but reduction or discontinuance may be for other reasons: to reduce expenses, to make room for a program the administration believes is more useful to the college, or to get rid of a troublesome activity or even one or more individuals. It is impossible to create a policy that is not dependent on individual judgment and therefore subject to possible manipulation. Hearings and court cases provide examples of faculty grievances over implementation of RIF policies.

Departmental, divisional, or area-of-instruction seniority is becoming as important as institutional seniority. The old rule that an instructor with a general credential was qualified to teach any subject or area of competency rarely applies now. And where credentials are not necessary for employment the subject or area of competency for which an instructor is employed to teach determines his seniority rights.

Complications arise when an instructor who has taught courses in other subjects or areas is teaching in a department with declining enrollment. An obvious example is the foreign languages department, where enrollment decline has been serious recently and where it is rare to find an instructor who is qualified to teach only one language. Teaching combinations are also common in the life, physical, and social sciences, some of which have also experienced a decline. In general, an instructor's rights depend a great deal on his assignments during his service. If he has taught more than one course in two or more disciplines, and if at the time he was not evaluated as inadequate in any of the subjects taught, he may acquire seniority rights in all the disciplines he has taught.

At Community College of Allegheny County (Pennsylvania), instructors holding a joint appointment and teaching more than one course in a department are considered members of that department with all privileges and responsibilities. In other colleges an instructor has membership in only one department, division, or learning area. In some colleges he retains the right to an assignment in another area in which he has taught ahead of any nontenured instructor. Other colleges give an instructor reasonable time in which to retrain for a position in another department or area.

The growth of multicampus systems introduces another variable. Seniority may be on a system-wide basis or restricted to the campus of employment. Under the former an instructor with higher seniority may bump an instructor with lower seniority on another campus. However, the administration usually retains the right to select which of two or more instructors with lower seniority are to be dismissed, whether on the same or on different campuses within the system. Nor, as at Allegheny, may a faculty member exercise his bumping right over tenured instructors "if it is possible to provide him with a full-time program through the elimination of part-time lectureships or overtime at his own college and then elsewhere in the college." Most community multicampus districts use the district-wide system, but Erie Community College (New York) uses campus seniority. State systems such as those in Hawaii, Minnesota, and New York use college seniority. In the CUNY system, seniority for tenured instructors is system-wide within the segment (community college or university).

A variety of rights has grown up around RIF. The policies always contain a requirement that the board notify the faculty member to be dismissed sometime (usually three to six months) before the end of the year in which the dismissal is to take place. However, since the procedure starts soon after it is determined that the staff must be reduced, those likely to be dismissed know or are notified early in the first semester. The most common official deadline dates are in March and April, with a few as early as December 15 (Minnesota).

Dismissed faculty members frequently have first claim if positions reopen. The Hawaii contract allows tenured faculty members who lose their positions due to a reduction in force to be placed on a preferential rehiring list, on the basis of their total years of service with the university, for a period of one year. Dismissed instructors retain rights to vacancies in their fields for three years at Allegheny, two years in Minnesota and New York. The Muskegon Community College (Michigan) and Moraine Valley Community College (Illinois) contracts contain no time limits on reassignment. Most contracts require that the dismissed faculty member apply for reassignment each year he has the right to do so. However, more and more are requiring that the board notify employees of vacancies by certified mail. Rehiring also follows seniority, the last fired, first rehired.

In a multicampus district the right extends to a vacancy in any district college. State and university systems also extend this right to a dismissed instructor, but it may be subject to the appointment prerogative of the receiving president. Colleges often make formal and informal efforts to help dismissed instructors find new positions, not only in their own systems but in other colleges. With the consent of the dismissed instructors they notify other college and university placement bureaus of the instructors' availability. Occasionally, they place advertisements in general and educational journals.

Faculty members recalled at Grays Harbor "retain all accrued benefits, such as sick leave and seniority [and] upon recall shall be placed at the next higher increment on the salary schedule than at the time of layoff and will retain their tenured status." Macomb County Community College reemployment does "not result in loss of status or credit for previous years of service," which means that the instructor will be placed at the increment on the salary schedule where he would be had he not been dismissed.

Under RIF, dismissal procedures depend heavily on seniority, the priority that comes from length of continuous service. This applies alike to policies in which faculty input is minimal and to those providing for a great deal of faculty participation. The early regulations governing large-scale reduction in force usually provided for separation on a simple college-wide seniority system. Thus, in 1942, when enrollment at Los Angeles City College declined from seven thousand to fifteen hundred, all faculty members were dismissed in May, and then, on the basis of a college-wide seniority roster prepared for the occasion, some were rehired before the opening of the fall semester.

Such a system based on last hired, first fired is not easily applied in colleges that today provide specialized courses governed by laws and regulations requiring specific rather than general degree qualifications for instructors and are subject to affirmative action policies. However, even where merit is indicated as a criterion, close examination of the policy or its implementation reveals that merit plays only a small part. Miami-Dade announced that "time of service would be immaterial in determining who would be retained and who would be dismissed," but of the fifty-four instructors released, fifty-one were on annual (nontenured) contract and three on continuing contract. The three "were in departments that suffered substantial student enrollment decreases, and their academic preparation was of such a specialized nature as to make it impractical to transfer them to other disciplines. . . ." Two of the annual contract personnel with long service were dismissed while a black instructor in the same department with one year of service was rehired in order for the college to maintain "the same percentage of black faculty members as it had before the cut-back was made."

Very few colleges provide severance pay to dismissed instructors. Oakland Community College (Michigan) grants one month's salary as severance compensation, while Lehigh County Community College (Pennsylvania) grants severance pay when instructors have not been notified six months in advance. Severance pay equal to 20 percent of unused sick leave up to a hundred days is given to every dismissed instructor in the Minnesota colleges. On termination of service, a teacher at Nassau Community College (New York) receives a cash payment equal to 25 percent of his unused sick leave up to a maximum of thirteen days.

In business and industry, allowing severance pay to employees laid off through no fault of their own is a common practice. It is likely that the practice will spread to the colleges. The growing practice of granting retired instructors lump-sum payments or credit for all or part of their unused sick leave may be the prelude to extending this benefit to dismissed instructors as well. This could be accomplished by college policy as at Nassau Community College or by state law making all instructors in good standing who are terminated, resign, or retire eligible for the payment of all or part of accrued sick leave. Waubonsee Community College (Illinois) extends lump-sum payments at retirement after fifteen years of service. For instructors terminated under RIF the fifteen year requirement would not be of much help, since most such instructors have fewer years of service at the time of dismissal; however, it usually is easy to extend a benefit to other classes of employees once a policy is established. For an instructor with short tenure, the Oakland lump-sum payment plan will be more beneficial than the sick leave payment.

Concern for the tenured and probationary instructors is in sharp contrast to the almost total absence of job protection for substitute, term assignment, adjunct, and part-time instructors.

When the need for reduction in force loomed, many administrators felt it would allow them to strengthen the faculty by eliminating weak instructors. With rare exception this has not happened. To attempt to do through RIF what should have been done through more direct means at the time an instructor was found to be inadequate is less than courageous and hardly a demonstration of good management. Nor have faculty leaders been able to seize the initiative in using RIF to dismiss the less competent. Their position seems to depend on the extent to which they can protect the entire staff. Moreover, it is easy to set up rules and procedures for determining who was hired first, who has tenure, and who must be let go through no fault of his own. In RIF, as in salary increments and many other procedures, seniority prevails. The college response to this force, generated by enrollment shifts beyond its control, has thus been to fall back on a time-honored—and court-approved—procedure: last hired, first fired.

Chapter Six

Expanding the Market

For decades curriculum in the community college has been centered on college-parallel and occupational courses. Recently these two program areas have been joined by a third. Listed under several headings—for example, adult education, community service, extended opportunity—these programs are presented for the benefit of special groups—handicapped persons, servicemen, prisoners, women with dependent children, and so on. Although they have little in common except that they are nontraditional, they can be grouped together as the most rapidly growing area of community college work.

    The many exhortations in favor of colleges expanding their nontraditional studies programs are based on the desirability of providing educational services to people who otherwise would not or could not benefit from the college. The premises are as follows. Excluded because of locale, low aptitude, lack of interest, or conflicting commitments, members of certain groups are nonetheless proper targets for the college that would serve everyone. Further, programs that attract nontraditional students help maintain growth in an era when the college-age population is leveling.

One in every ten persons in the United States is now sixty-five years old or over, an increase of more than 600 percent since 1900. Moreover, the increase in life expectancy is accompanied by a lowering of retirement age, giving older people many years of leisure time that, if not used well, can be years of loneliness and frustration (Carlson, 1973).

Many prestigious organizations and individuals recognize the need to extend educational opportunities to retired people. The White House Conference on Aging (Helling and Bauer, 1972) sets forth several long-range goals of education for the aged. These include helping older people fulfill their potential, develop abilities uniquely available in the later years, assist society in the utilization of these abilities, and serve as models for the oncoming generations. Institutions are responsible for making special provisions for delivering educational programs to "hidden populations" of older people, usually nonparticipants, isolated from the mainstream of community services.

Community colleges are beginning to respond to this need. A 1973 survey of ninety-eight California community colleges lists twenty-three colleges that offer classes or programs specifically for retired persons (Korim, 1974b). Similar programs can be found in community colleges across the country. Services for older adults are generally provided in three ways: free or reduced tuition for the aged, special classes or programs for people who are about to retire or are already retired, and curricula to train manpower to work with the aged.

A national study conducted by the American Association of Community and Junior Colleges (AACJC) and reported by Korim (1974b) indicates that offering free or reduced tuition to the elderly is widespread. Of 1113 institutions responding, 147 colleges in 43 states provide this service. The following descriptions give an idea of the scope of these programs. All are provided by the AACJC report with the exception of one program whose source is listed under the program description.

Honolulu Community College (Hawaii) sponsors the Hawaii State Senior Center, a walk-in multipurpose facility devoted to the needs of the aged for adjustment and constructive use of leisure time. It includes a health screening program, an information-referral service, and both basic educational and recreational activities. The center is funded by a grant from the Hawaii Commission on Aging, Title III, Older Americans Act.

North Hennepin State Junior College (Minnesota) operates a Seniors-on-Campus program that provides a wide variety of college courses for older adults, such as Senior Power, Preparing Income Tax, and Indoor Gardening. Tuition is free and transportation is provided by the college. The program is funded by a grant from the Minnesota Governor's Citizens Council on Aging, Title III, Older Americans Act.

Snead State Junior College (Alabama) operates project Do Unto Others (DUO) and Retired Senior Volunteer Program (RSVP), which provide opportunities for elderly citizens to volunteer services in their areas of interest. Activities range from writing letters for hospitalized patients to aiding in community center activities. They are funded by an RSVP grant from ACTION, with supplementary funds from various community organizations. (RSVP programs were operating in ten states as of June 30, 1973.)

Clark County Community College (Nevada) operates a Meals-on-Wheels program that serves approximately 130 older adults each day. Students from the college drive the trucks, participate in food preparation, undertake clean-up and service work, and conduct social activities. Meals are delivered to four sites and to twenty homebound people. The program is funded by a grant from the Nevada Division of Aging Services, Department of Health, Welfare, and Rehabilitation.

New York City Community College (New York) provides educational experiences at community senior centers. A unique aspect of this program is the opportunity for six community college students to gain experience in administering a program for older people. It is funded by a grant from the New York State Office for the Aging, Title III, Older Americans Act.

St. Petersburg Junior College (Florida) operates a program for older adults living at the Top of the World Condominium, a complex of buildings in Pinellas County, Florida, an area with a large elderly population. Courses include yoga, creative writing, parapsychology, and condominium botany (Cole, 1973).

These five programs take into account the special needs of the elderly as identified by Carlson (1973) in a survey of over two thousand retired persons living in California. He concludes that many of the aged find taking tests threatening because they accept the traditional (and largely false) assumption that old people have poor memories and cannot learn. To allay this fear, most of the classes for the elderly are noncredit. Moreover, Carlson emphasizes that older people want classes that will utilize their competence and knowledge as active participants rather than passive listeners. Finally, he indicates that the classes take the physical limitations of their students into account by providing convenient locations or transportation.

In addition to reduced tuition rates and special programs for older citizens, community colleges are beginning to offer AA degrees or certificates to prepare manpower to work with the elderly. A survey of 1137 community colleges, originally conducted in October 1972 and updated in March 1974, shows that forty-two of the surveyed colleges offered training programs in the field of aging. Twenty-four colleges offered associate degree programs in such fields as nursing, home administration, geriatrics, gerontology, and home-care management. Also, certificate programs or short courses relating to aging occupations were offered by twenty-one colleges (Korim, 1974a).

Another group with special educational problems is military personnel, whose needs are described by Betts: "The key educational problem a serviceman confronts is forced mobility. During his tour of duty his educational experiences may be frequently interrupted through temporary duty reassignment or relocation. . . . Seldom is he in one location long enough to meet all degree and residency requirements at one institution. Frequently he has difficulty transferring credits between institutions. In addition, his previous experiences, both in and out of service, may project him beyond the normal requirements of an entering student. He may have opportunity, on- or off-duty, to pursue special educational opportunities sponsored by military educational agencies. Conversely, there may be instances when he may find himself behind the entering student" (1973, p. 1).

To meet these nontraditional requirements the Servicemen's Opportunity College (SOC) concept was developed in 1972 by the Department of Defense and the AACJC, working cooperatively through the Task Force on Extending Educational Opportunities for Servicemen. SOC is a community college that provides assistance as outlined by Betts.

Entrance requirements are liberal with a high school diploma or GED certificate generally being adequate. In colleges not restricted by law, even the above requirements may be waived for promising students. Courses are offered on the base, in the evenings, on weekends, and at other nontraditional times. Nontraditional means are provided for servicemen to complete courses when their education is interrupted by military obligations. Special academic remedial help is available through tutorial services, counseling, and Predischarge Education Programs (PREP). Maximum credit is allowed toward the AA degree for educational experiences obtained in the Armed Services or at other institutions. Credit is granted for appropriate United States Armed Forces Institute courses and through the College Level Examination Program, College Proficiency Examination Program, and institutional "challenge" examinations. In addition, servicemen are generally exempted from required health and physical education courses. Credit may be granted for other educational experiences in accordance with the American Council on Education's 1968 publication, *A Guide to the Evaluation of Educational Experiences in the Armed Services,* [Turner, 1968] or by the Commission on the Accreditation of Service Experiences evaluation service. Residency requirements are adaptable to the mobility of servicemen with at least one of the following degree options offered: a contract which allows courses from other institutions to be applied toward degree requirements, complete elimination of residency requirements, or exemption from requirements specified by law. A local advisory council is established to aid the college in carrying out its program for servicemen.

The college must maintain its commitment to servicemen previously enrolled even if it discontinues its status as an soc. These policies are publicized through the college catalogue or by other appropriate means.

One community college is unique in the field of armed forces education, having been established by the military itself. This is Community College of the Air Force, established in 1971 with the idea of gaining formal educational recognition for military technical training. At its seven campuses the college integrates the education airmen receive through Air Force schools, field training detachments, supervised work experience, and off-duty education into a career study program culminating in a Career Education Certificate. The certificate is offered in eight general areas: administration and management, aircraft maintenance, communications, crafts and trades, distribution services, electromechanics, health care, and public services (*Community College of the Air Force*, 1973). This program serves to attract volunteers, which, since the abolition of the draft, has become an increasingly important consideration.

The educational programs in American prisons have a long history of development as described by Adams (1973). From the 1700s through the 1800s education in American prisons focused on teaching the Scriptures. Gradually literacy training was added, and by the end of the 1800s both academic and vocational training were well established in the prisons of the more progressive states. In the 1930s and 1940s the academic and vocational programs of large state and federal prisons were substantially improved, and counseling services were added. At this point academic training was extended beyond basic literacy to help students prepare for high school equivalency examinations, and by the 1950s the challenge was to provide postsecondary education. This was done at first by correspondence courses, but by the mid-fifties extension courses taught at the prison were introduced. This concept proved popular and is still growing.

Adams and Connolly (1971) report a study of state correctional systems conducted in the late 1960s, which disclosed that thirty-one of the forty-nine systems cooperated with colleges and universities in providing educational programs to inmates. Programs included live instruction, televised instruction, and the college furlough in which inmate students are bused to college by day and returned to prison at night. One of the most influential prisoner education programs was at San Quentin Prison. It was originally launched amid much fanfare as a pilot project heading toward a four-year liberal arts college behind bars, but at the end of two years it was decided that a two-year program offered by the College of Marin (California) would be more feasible. Because of early publicity, this project emerged as a model, spawning similar projects in Oregon (the Newgate Project) and in Washington, D.C. (the Federal City College— Lorton Programs).

Another program involving San Quentin seeks to help parolees and probationers through a peer-tutoring approach (Frankel and others, 1973). Correctional science majors, called counselor aides, at Yuba College (California) are paired with students on parole from San Quentin and students on probation in a one-to-one tutorial program. The students, who must meet entrance requirements and enroll for credit, receive individualized academic tutoring from the counselor aides and in return help them understand the realities of life behind bars. The success of this unusual program is due in part to the fact that "correctional science majors and tutors [parolees and probationers] function as a family—one in which the two groups try to positively reinforce one another, reduce frustration, and form nonthreatening interpersonal relationships" (p. 57).

As reported in the Adams and Connolly (1971) survey described above, some colleges are beginning to rely heavily on educational technology. The use of technology is illustrated by the program operated by Mercer County Community College (New Jersey) at Trenton State Prison, Leesburg Prison, the Leesburg Farm, and Rahway Prison (Greenfield, 1972). In 1972 the 270 students at these prisons were taught by the Mercer County Community College Prison Education network, which uses telecture and electrowriter units. The telecture transmits lectures given at the college to each of the four prisons simultaneously, making it possible for inmates to participate in discussions both with each other and with the professor. The electrowriter projects illustrations, notes, and other material to all the prisons simultaneously on an overhead screen at each institution. Students may also send written material back to the college through this machine. The telecture and electrowriter units are used for two of the three lectures given each week; the third is given in person by the instructor. The use of technology has generally been successful, although in vocational programs, more "hands-on" training is necessary.

As Adams and Connolly point out, the special characteristics of community colleges make them among the best suited of all institutions of higher learning to conduct educational programs for prisoners. They are open-door institutions, so admission problems are few. Their offerings are varied, and they are experienced in dealing with disadvantaged people. Finally, they are readily accessible to most jails and prisons. Although it is not possible to judge the effects of these programs without more data, it is evident that their aims are humanitarian in that they attempt to create an atmosphere of rehabilitation, rather than retribution, behind prison bars.

Drug abuse programs are similar to prisoner education programs, not only because they often deal with similar populations but because they too are aimed at rehabilitation rather than punishment. These programs have been established in recognition of the fact that the misuse of drugs is a widespread and serious problem. It has been estimated that heroin alone is used by more than one-half million Americans whose habit costs the nation several billion dollars a year in property losses (Ognibene, 1972). Studies of college students reported by Yolles (1971) suggest that drug experimentation is part of college life. Surveys of selected college populations during the late 1960s showed that 2 to 9 percent had tried LSD, up to 21 percent had tried amphetamines, and up to 25 percent had tried barbiturates.

Educational programs for the prevention of drug abuse or the rehabilitation of drug addicts derive from a powerful faith in the ability of education to prevent or change undesirable behavior. Although no data exist concerning the total number or location of community college–sponsored programs, some drug treatment and educational centers are described below.

Kirkwood Community College (Iowa), which is responsible for community adult education, offers a series of lectures on various drugs, drug laws, and community involvement, as well as an in-service training program for K-12 teachers (Casse and others, 1972).

Oakland Community College (Michigan) has a drug-abuse prevention and treatment center that has been described as a comprehensive model to be emulated by other colleges. Serving two hundred to three hundred people weekly, it carries out activities such as in-service training courses for college personnel; a referral program encouraging other agencies to send drug abusers to the center for counseling; speaking engagements for community groups, providing basic research publications to the public at minimal cost; and a drug-assistant program which trains paraprofessionals through a thirty-hour program and a short internship. Eventually an AA degree in counseling is planned (Jalkanen, 1972).

St. Clair College of Applied Arts and Technology (Ontario, Canada) is a community college–operated residence center for drug abuse rehabilitation. The college sponsors Twin Valley Farms, which enrolled twenty students in 1973 and is based on an educational rather than a mental-health model. The latter assumes that the drug abuser needs rehabilitation, that he needs to relearn social relationships and other skills that he once possessed. The educational model, on the other hand, assumes that, because of his total involvement with drugs, the drug abuser has never learned appropriate social skills and that his education must therefore start from the beginning. Twin Valley attempts to establish a learning climate where students can acquire social as well as academic skills by using both to satisfy the basic needs for food, shelter, and clothing. Classroom learning, which is granted college credit, is implemented in practical activities. Of the twelve students originally living at the school, eleven have become full-time college students or members of the labor force. The program's initial success seems due to its philosophy, training techniques, and low student-teacher ratio, all of which give the student skills and confidence to reenter society (Pietrofesa and others, 1973).

Nassau Community College (New York) offers a program similar in intent to the one at Oakland Community College, since both are geared to drug abuse prevention and rehabilitation. All students are required to take a basic drug-education course. In addition, the college has developed videotapes, pamphlets, and in-service courses for community education.

The rehabilitation program is two-pronged. Students with drug problems are counseled through the Department of Student Personnel Services, and classes for ex–drug addicts are given at Topic House, Nassau County's Drug Rehabilitation Residential Center. A preliminary evaluation of this part of the program for 1969–1970 was encouraging. Individuals in the program had a higher rate of staying off drugs and of employment stability than those who did not take any classes (Veselak and others, 1971). As these descriptions suggest, extensive data do not exist regarding the effectiveness of community college programs in preventing drug abuse or in rehabilitating drug abusers. Questions need to be answered not only about the methods of these programs, but, more basically, about their goals. Arguing that education alone cannot change behavior, especially behavior that may be habitual or that may be encouraged by a subculture, critics have claimed that drug education can never prevent drug abuse, therefore it should have more modest aims. Ognibene (1972), in assessing the failure of heavily funded federal education programs in preventing the endemic spread of drugs, commented that such programs should lower their sights; rather than try to prevent drug abuse, they should be content with giving the public accurate information and avoiding the spread of misinformation, which might backfire, such as in antimarijuana campaigns.

Rural colleges are an important part of the community college scene. Sixty percent of the community colleges in the United States have enrollments of 1500 or less and serve districts with populations of one hundred thousand or less (Myran and MacLeod, 1972). These small institutions are prototypes of the do-everything college, since they offer an extraordinary array of programs aimed at the needs of diverse groups. A varied curriculum is necessary because, located in sparsely settled areas, rural community colleges must function somewhat like one-room schoolhouses, that is, they must serve many small groups of people with differing needs. The comprehensive nature of rural colleges is illustrated by Flathead Valley Community College (Montana) (Van Dyne, 1973a). In addition to its regular transfer and occupational programs, Flathead serves about seven hundred adult students through a series of part-time and short-term programs. These people include everybody from executives of the local aluminum company to the Blackfoot Indians on a reservation just beyond its district. Examples of the diverse kinds of program offered are a five-session marriage-counseling course instituted at the request of a local judge, adult education courses ranging from rock hounding and body conditioning to income tax preparation and horseshoeing, workshops and courses requested by local unions and businesses to train people in skills needed by the organizations, and ethnic studies programs for Indians on two major reservations and on campus.

As the Flathead example suggests, a major emphasis for the rural community college is in community service. Two other focal points for the rural curriculum are vocational education and cultural preservation and uplift. Vocational education is becoming essential to combat rural poverty, which may be more pervasive than urban poverty.

Community college occupational programs are an important means of fighting this poverty, since they help attract industry to rural areas by training potential employees. Delaware Technical Community College (Delaware), for example, illustrates how this may be done (Astarita, 1973). Located in a rural area of eighty thousand people where over 10 percent of the population is either unemployed, underemployed, or living below the poverty level, Delaware Tech has placed over 85 percent of its graduates within forty-five miles of the college at an average starting salary of seven thousand to eight thousand dollars per year. In addition, it has trained hard-core unemployed as heavy equipment operators, construction workers, and truck drivers. About 350 people have been employed through this program over a four-year period. Finally, Delaware Tech has attracted industry to its community; the availability of Delaware Tech training facilities was an instrumental factor in the National Cash Register company's decision to locate in southern Delaware.

At colleges that serve a particular ethnic group, efforts in community service and in occupational education go hand-in-hand with efforts to preserve the local culture. This is particularly true for colleges with American Indian populations. Some programs aimed at particular ethnic groups are summarized here.

Navajo College (Arizona) implements the community service idea by preserving and transmitting the Navajo heritage and by helping the people develop the economic resources of their land. Accordingly, the college tries to employ only Navajos in its construction activities and in its instructional program. Non-Navajo employees are replaced whenever qualified Navajos are available (Cohen, 1972).

DQU College (California), located in the middle of the Sacramento Valley, was organized by and for American Indians and Chicanos. It offers the "usual spectrum of undergraduate courses, but all emphasize Native American and Chicano culture. In addition, the college has developed its own brand of higher education: students learn history from medicine men, agriculture from ranch foreman, [and] small-business administration from successful entrepreneurs." The college had only a hundred students in 1973, but plans to expand to four colleges with a total enrollment of fifteen hundred students ("DQU: A New Breed," 1973).

The Old Sun campus of Mount Royal College (Alberta, Canada) serves the Blackfoot Indians. As the first institution of higher education established on a Canadian Indian reservation, Old Sun tries to take the culture of the Indian into account in every aspect of its program. Thus, whenever possible, events on campus follow the Indian custom of being part of family activity. Also, the achievement of artificial deadlines and the translation of Indian ideas into "good English" are deemphasized (Fogg, 1972).

Mountain Empire Community College (Virginia) preserves and teaches the heritage of mountain folk. This commitment is evidenced at the semiannual Home Crafts Day, during which older craftsmen demonstrate and teach skills once considered essential for survival in the mountains, such as shoeing mules, quilting, carding wool, and building barns. Other activities geared to cultural preservation are: field work assignments during which students work directly with local craftsmen; preparation of a record album of local music; apple-butter-making; and the development of folklife and culture seminars for local public school teachers (Turnage and Moore, 1973).

Like most educational institutions, rural community colleges face major problems. Rural areas, particularly if they are very remote and isolated, generally do not offer an intellectual climate attractive to the university-oriented educator (Sine and Pesci, 1973). This fact, as well as the lower salaries paid, makes it difficult for these colleges to attract and hold faculty. In addition, there is the even greater problem of logistics (Powless, 1971). Since rural colleges often serve large and sparsely populated territories, getting the student to campus is difficult. The solution lies in getting the campus to the student. The California Rural Consortium and Coordinating Council for Higher Education has prepared a report (Hall, 1973) showing delivery systems that can be used.

Correspondence programs deliver material to the student at home, where he reads instruction, studies, and takes exams. Recently the University of California at Davis pioneered a newspaper course by providing installments of a humanities class in the daily paper. Mobile units, or traveling classrooms, take counseling and instruction to remote areas. These are currently used in occupational training. Televised instruction in conjunction with community study centers provides at least minimal face-to-face contact between students. And external degree programs allow students to meet degree requirements without attending classes or residing at the college. Several California community colleges now offer these programs.

An important delivery system not mentioned by the Rural Consortium is the use of rural outposts. Under this system, the central campus is either nonexistent or unimportant for instructional purposes. Rather, courses are offered wherever the people are and in whatever facilities are available. Rural outposts are used on a statewide basis in Vermont (Parker and Vecchitto, 1973). Vermont Community College has no central campus at all; its classes are held in high schools, churches, youth centers, and other facilities in which residents can pursue college work close to home. The quality of instruction and student achievement are monitored closely. Students and administrators evaluate teachers, and degrees are earned only by students who can demonstrate a predetermined number of competencies.

Whatcom College (Washington) uses a similar outpost system, as does Central Arizona Community College. The latter serves about fifty Indians on its central campus and about six hundred Indians through outposts in various parts of the state. These outposts include the Gila River Career Center, which offers educational programs to the adult disadvantaged members of the Gila River Indian Community; classes for Head Start Indian teachers throughout Arizona, even at the bottom of the Havasupai Canyon in the Grand Canyon; classes for mental health aides at Desert Willows near Tucson; and English as a Second Language/Basic Education programs at the Gila River and Papago Reservations (Personal communication with Don Pence, January 1974).

The choice of a particular delivery system depends on the situation, including the number of people to be served, their geographic distribution, and the services to be offered. However, no matter what their method, rural programs are reaching previously neglected students.

Another group that is beginning to get special attention is the physically handicapped. Although little has been written about community college programs for the physically handicapped, a major document was completed in 1971 (Educational Programs for the Handicapped), which describes the situation in California and also provides guidelines for establishing programs.

Physically handicapped students attending California community colleges include the orthopedically handicapped, the deaf and hard of hearing, the blind and partially sighted, and persons with speech, language, and communication disorders. The number of handicapped students is increasing. "For the 1970–1971 academic year, enrollment of handicapped students in California community college vocational education programs soared to 51,428 as compared to the 1969–1970 enrollment of 10,514. This phenomenal growth is expected to continue" (*Educational Programs for the Handicapped*, 1971, p. 5).

Funding for the programs comes from three major sources aside from district resources: the Vocational Education Act of 1968 (Public Law 90-576), state funds, and contributions from private organizations. The Vocational Education Act (vea) mandates that 10 percent of all Vocational Education Part B funds be earmarked specifically for the physically handicapped. This allotment may be used to purchase, lease, or rent equipment; pay the salaries and support services of instructors and counselors; and make building modifications. One year after the act went into effect, a nationwide survey of building modifications designed for students in wheelchairs was conducted (Tuscher and Fox, 1971). About one-third of the 168 community colleges contacted had curbs or steps between the parking lots and college facilities. Only 22 percent of the colleges had modified lavatory facilities and 13 percent had lowered drinking fountains. However, about one-half of the colleges did have ramps or reserved parking places. Those institutions that offered modified facilities were attended by more physically handicapped students than those that did not.

The second source of funding—the state—varies its requirements from state to state. In California, for example, the Education Code provides $17,260 per class, minus the district contribution. However, in California, state funds may be spent only for minors, whereas vea funds may be used for both minors and adults.

The third source of funding—contributions from private organizations, such as the Lions, Rotary, and Kiwanis clubs—is detailed in a guide prepared by the American Association for

Health, Physical Education, and Recreation (*Guide for Financial Assistance* . . . , 1973). They offer funds for such items as special lighting, Braille books, and specially designed study carrels.

In addition to exploring funding possibilities, other guidelines should be followed in setting up the program. Community need must be analyzed; staff capabilities must be reviewed; procedures, programs, and publicity must be worked out. These steps were followed by the community college system in Virginia, where a master plan was developed (*Identification and Accommodation of Disadvantaged and Handicapped Students* . . . , 1971) to determine the potential number of handicapped students by college region, identify means of providing for these students, and examine numbers being served by specialized instructional offerings. On the basis of these data, specialized programs were planned.

An analysis of staff capabilities is another important consideration in program planning since, as with any program, the instructor is a key factor in its ultimate success or failure. Fasteau (1972), an instructor of handicapped students at Cerritos College (California), outlined the major faculty functions. The primary responsibility is to support the handicapped person through advising, testing, tutoring, or giving moral support. The faculty is also an important source of publicity, both in recruiting students and in explaining the program to the community.

As they identify community needs and evaluate funding possibilities and staff capabilities, college personnel must think about the kind of program they will offer—primarily service-oriented, curriculum-oriented, or a combination of the two. A service-oriented program encourages the handicapped student to participate in the same courses as other students, but offers him special services such as priority registration, housing, transportation, readers, and attendant care. The curriculum-oriented program involves course work specifically aimed at the handicapped. This might include courses such as the "Psychological Aspects of Disability," "Speech Therapy," or "Oral and Manual Communication for the Deaf." It was concluded in *Educational Programs for the Handicapped* that the most effective programs combine special services with special curriculum. Several colleges in California have developed this kind of program.

One of the oldest community college programs for the physically handicapped is offered by Williamsport Area Community College (Pennsylvania). The school was founded in 1919 to help disabled veterans of World War I who needed vocational retraining. According to its president, Carl (1972), the most innovative part of the curriculum is a three-week vocational diagnostic program. After a battery of physical, academic, and vocational tests, the student is encouraged to visit over fifty different vocational classes and choose the occupation that seems most appealing. If his physical record does not disqualify him, the student is given a three-day trial in the shop or lab he has chosen and, later, a number of small jobs representative of the work to be learned. On completion of this assignment the student is placed in three or four similar work trials, and, on the basis of these, makes his occupational-training selection. During the 1971–1972 school year the college had 185 physically handicapped students enrolled in thirty-seven different occupational courses.

The facilities and curriculum at Wytheville Community College (Virginia) have been described by Tuscher and Fox (1971). The program is service oriented, counseling is provided for all handicapped students, readers and individualized tests are available for the visually handicapped, speech therapy is offered to students with communication problems, and transportation is provided for students who need it.

The program at Central Piedmont College (North Carolina) is quite similar to the one at Wytheville. No special courses are given, but counseling, special elevators and ramps, readers, recorded books, and large-type class notes are available. Enrollment in this program expanded from 74 students in 1971 to 350 students in 1973 (Personal communication with C. S. Boukouralas, January 1974).

In contrast to Wytheville and Central Piedmont colleges, Wright College (S. Friedman, 1974), one of the City Colleges of Chicago, planned a curriculum-oriented program to be introduced during spring 1974. Three courses were to be offered for the blind and visually impaired: Personal Management, stressing homemaking skills such as meal planning, budgeting, shopping, and the use of a sewing machine; Braille I, an introductory course emphasizing note-taking and the development of reading skills; and Understanding and Accepting Visual Impairment, designed to help the blind or visually impaired person and his family adjust to the difficulties that accompany loss of sight.

It would be helpful to have more of these descriptions and some evaluative data concerning programs for the physically handicapped in community colleges. The data that are available suggest that these programs, with the help of VEA money, are expanding and will become another community college responsibility.

At this point, it is appropriate to examine the implications of assuming new responsibilities. It seems clear that unless resources are unlimited (which they are not), a college cannot expand its functions indefinitely. Rather, a decision to offer programs in one area, whether for senior citizens, prison inmates, the handicapped, or any other category, will eventually lead to a reduction of emphasis in another area. Thus, several questions for the future role of the community college are posed: Who decides how the resources will be allocated, which programs will be supported, and which will not? Will the decisions be made by the customers of the college (the students), by the instructors through collective bargaining contracts, by administrators, by government officials, or by university professors and others involved in community college research? Will economic influences such as changing job requirements or the competition from proprietary schools influence decisions? What about political pressures reflected in government spending priorities or teacher militancy? What will be the effect of various social phenomena such as changing life styles? Undoubtedly all will have some effect in shaping the future community college role, but some voices will be louder than others.

Chapter Seven

Community Development: Impossible Dream?

The programs described in Chapter Six represent only a portion of the nontraditional areas in which two-year colleges are getting involved. Many others fall under the catchall heading, community services. Although community service has been recognized as a proper function since the publication of Bogue's *Community College* in 1950, only in the past few years has it gained extensive interest. Harlacher's *Community Dimension of the Community College* (1969) was a benchmark since which an accelerated emphasis on this area has developed.

In a speech to the 1974 AACJC national convention, Pifer articulated a new community college function—that of coordinating agent for all other community service agencies: "Indeed, I'm going to make the outrageous suggestion that community colleges should start thinking about themselves from now on only secondarily as a sector of higher education and regard as their primary role community leadership. . . . Not least, they can become the hub of a network of institutions and community agencies—the high schools, industry, the church, voluntary agencies, youth groups, even the prison system and the courts

—utilizing their educational resources and, in turn, becoming a resource for them" (*The Improvement of Community Life* . . . , 1974). Almost simultaneously the AACJC board of directors issued a strongly worded statement corroborating that function: "The Mission of the American Association of Community and Junior Colleges is to provide an organization for national leadership of community-based postsecondary education" (Gleazer, 1974a).

The spokesmen for the two-year colleges seem to be urging institutional leaders to stake out a ground now pending the imminent state-level coordination of all postsecondary education that will see the role of two-year and four-year colleges and universities clearly demarcated. Or perhaps they are reacting to the changing enrollment patterns, which reveal increasing percentages of adults matriculating by rushing to the front of the moving crowd and shouting, "Follow me!" Articulating a new mission is also a way of denying the failure of an old one—general education, for example, where the community colleges have done no better than the secondary schools in fostering literacy, taste, and respect for traditions except among students whose entire social milieu supports this form of enculturation. Whatever the reason, the term *community service* is in the process of being modified to *community development*.

The proponents of community development are overjoyed with their newly won recognition. McClusky (1974) says, "To anyone aware of the long-standing marginal status of ACCE [Adult Continuing and Community Education], the commitment of the community college to adult education and community service is a triumph of educational achievement. Protected by this mandate, it does not have to beg, apologize, or depend on the crumbs of support and status left over from the remainder of the institution's program. It is no longer a third-class stepchild, but has finally become a full-fledged, equal partner in the educational enterprise" (p. 22).

Has it? It will take more than pronouncements by national leaders to make it so. Community development is a noble educational aim, but much stands between the institutions and this ideal. How can community services be funded equitably?

How can this function be reconciled with other college services, especially the instructional program? How will other community service agencies take to the competition for funding and clients? What are the chances for community services to move to a central position in colleges that were organized and staffed to perform other services?

Harlacher's book (1969) is a good place to begin an analysis of these questions. He states that the community college is receptive to the idea of community development because it is "a relatively new segment of American education, . . . unencrusted with tradition, unfettered by a rigid history, eager for adventure" (pp. 8–9). He feels that because of "its uniqueness, freedom from tradition, and dynamic qualities" (p. 9) the community college, as opposed to the four-year institution, can establish valuable community-service activities. Lavish in his praise, Harlacher sees the college as "disinterested in terms of the community power structure, [with] no profit motive . . . , no axe to grind. . . . It is the unified force that casts aside red tape, apathy, jealousies, and asks what the community problems are and how 'all of us together [can] solve them' " (p. 9). Martin Cohen (1972) suggests too that the community-services programs of community colleges represent an ideal in educational services because they are "unhampered by the imposition of grades, hours, credits, and credential standards by agencies outside the college" (p. 1). He sees this freedom to devise programs that further the intellectual, esthetic, spiritual, and practical life of the community as a positive force.

Such advocacy is not unusual; each of the many functions included under the rubric of the community college has fervid proponents; one might expect community services to have its corps of supporters. However, a close reading of the claims made on behalf of community development reveals several problems. For one thing, there is a gulf between the supporters' rhetoric and the perceptions of college planners and leaders. Most community colleges are just not that receptive to genuine community development. Except for a few isolated cases, the community dimension of the community college is narrow, inchoate, and removed from the mainstream of college operations. And it enjoys the dubious distinction of being the function least coherently defined, least amenable to assessment.

The advocates of community development usually recognize the gap between current programs and the ideal. Even Harlacher acknowledges that community services are somewhat less than equal to transfer, occupational, and counseling and guidance functions. But he feels obstacles to the development of that function will be overcome as soon as administrators and faculty members accept community development as a major function. In 1969 his optimism led him to predict that "the community college will increasingly utilize its catalytic capabilities to assist its community in the solution of basic educational, economic, political, and social problems" (p. 90). But he could point to only a few scattered examples as a basis for such development: colleges offering advisory services to small businesses, those organizing community councils, and those conducting one-shot community surveys.

Gleazer (1974a) inadvertently reveals that little has changed in the intervening years. In announcing the "new mission," he offers a child-care center at one college, a black community advisory committee at another, a college renting space to small businesses, and some cooperative work-experience programs as examples of the links that are developing between community colleges and their larger communities. Other evidence is provided by a survey made in preparation for a 1974 conference on community services (Personal communication with M. Turnage, April 1974) wherein the presidents of a hundred colleges were asked to provide information on their colleges' "contribution to community development." Their responses described such programs as off-campus courses for paraplegics, an adult education series sponsored cooperatively by a college and two local school districts, and allowing the local Chamber of Commerce to operate an "industrial briefing center" in a college board room.

The slow development of community services may be attributed to several problems, one being the plurality of communities. Community means commonality, shared experience, a convergent viewpoint; however, each of us is a member of a dozen or more communities—religious, social, ethnic, age—any one of which may become significant to us at any time, depending on the issue at hand. If a zoning change is imminent we rally with our neighbors; if there is a slur on our church we are as one with our coreligionists across town. As Spiegel (1972) puts it, "We move in an urban world composed of multiple 'communities of interest.'"

In addition, the colleges themselves fail to form a single community. Harlacher says that community-service programs offer the logical vehicle for joining the college with the life of its district or service area. He speaks of "college" and "district" as though they were living entities when, in fact, they are comprised of people—people whose diversities are much more pronounced than their similarities. There is little common meaning, few shared beliefs, within the colleges. There is not even an episodic approach to community wherein groups coalesce, degenerate, and reform around successive interests and issues.

The community college is less a community than it is an institution, a term that suggests self-perpetuation but not cohesive goals. On rare occasions a sense of community can be discerned within a college—such as on the first day of classes when a feeling of common experience is in the air or during accreditation or when the college is under attack from the outside. Otherwise, it is an aggregation of people with their own inconsistent definitions of what the college is about. "Community college" may be a misnomer; the institution might more aptly be named "commuter college"—a place where administrators, instructors, counselors, and students come, interact together within defined roles, and depart, each to his own ventures.

The closest approximation to a community of interest in a college centers on the instructional program—the courses, the teaching techniques. This is the function that dominates the thinking of the staff, with all else—community services in particular—relegated to a peripheral position. Writers on the community college perpetuate the attitude: Monroe (1972) warns, "In serving the community, the community college needs to guard against the danger of dissipating its resources by trying to perform so many different services for the community that it may not be able to perform its primary task of providing the students with quality education" (pp. 31–32). Lombardi (1974) concurs, "The educational aspects of our responsibilities in community services must be emphasized; for this is where we can contribute the most. Education is our mission, our reason for existence. It is not envisioned that our regular collegiate program—traditional courses, grades, credentials and degrees —be transformed, subordinated or eliminated" (p. 7). Perhaps this is as it should be—the college is foremost an institution for instruction—but it leaves the advocates of community development out in the cold.

Staff members' perceptions of their role tend to slow the move toward a new emphasis. Ideally the entire college staff would be involved as planners and participators in community development. But the current generation of instructors was hired originally to teach American history, English composition, and data processing in classrooms on a campus. The past few years have seen them buffeted by demands to change their attitudes and methods to accommodate nontraditional students, to adopt new media, and to become "relevant" and "accountable." Shall we now expect them to abandon their classrooms and go out to work as agents of community uplift? The answer sometimes given is that the instructional program should be subordinate to community development—but this is easier said than done. One college attempted to assign 20 percent of all faculty members' time to the community-services director, but its effort foundered on the twin rocks of faculty disinclination and administrative rivalry (personal communication with M. Turnage, April 1974).

Most community-service directors skirt the problem of intracollege competition and entrenched ideas by building their programs with tenureless, part-time staff members, paid by extramural funds. This makes it appear as though the services will remain pointed at community problems. Perhaps so, but it also ensures that the programs remain peripheral. Elsner (1974) says of the dilemma: "The educational dollar, formerly set aside for instructional purposes, must stretch for community action, theater, recreation, films, cultural events, consumer protection, legal aid, etc. . . . . While the public tolerance for general expenditures in education is high, areas like community service programs appear to be equally accommodated; yet when resources are scarce, the public, at least represented by our board of trustees, is anxious to scrutinize ancillary programs" (pp. 19 and 23). In short, when something must be cut, the nontraditional goes first.

The community college is not a house for independently functioning agents of community uplift. It is a school, it is organized and administered like a school, and it does things the way schools do them. Despite its recent efforts to recruit students by sending mobile units into shopping center parking lots, despite its offering a few courses off campus, and despite its opening the swimming pool to neighborhood children on Saturdays, it remains a school—operationally, fiscally, and in the eyes of its constituency. Regardless of the label, community service courses differ from the standard course fare only in that they arise ad hoc and accordingly do not claim space in the college catalog or on student transcripts. Otherwise, they are much like the transfer, vocational, and other curricula; they have teachers and students acting within defined roles.

Cultural and recreational activities off campus and noncredit courses are the stuff of which community services is made. Despite the pleas to coordinate all service agencies, one sees only more spectator events, more short courses over the horizon— hardly the community college as a total service directed toward community uplift. The community-services director who wants to establish specific objectives that reach beyond the usual cultural, recreational, and educational services has little recourse within the college or the community. The objectives of the community development program will reflect the interpretation that college leaders give it. If they wish merely to allow members of the broader community to attend college-sponsored events and receive disconnected educational services, then the number of participants is the measure of success. These are process goals. Whether or not they lead to tangible products in the sense of community development is beyond the scope of the community services director.

Programs in a few colleges have progressed toward co-ordinated community development. In 1970, Harrisburg Area Community College (Pennsylvania) established an Urban Development Institute that provides consultant services and specially tailored contract courses to governmental, business, and civic organizations, and otherwise participates cooperatively with numerous agencies by offering college assistance in administering grants and conducting community surveys (personal communication with M. Turnage, Feb. 1974). Although the Institute involves only a small portion of the college staff, it is a beginning. Most important, it has definite purpose and serves as an example of community service that is well related to educational activities.

If a college were to offer itself as an integrated community development agency, what form might it take? A unified approach would demand an orchestration of programs so that the entire college would be concerned with crucial issues relating to the community. It would demand a distinct image of the college as an agency that regularly surveys the community on a number of important issues. It would require social science instructors to see an educational value in the routine collection of voter information by their students; life sciences instructors to revise their courses to include the students' assessment of levels of pollution in community air and waters; physical science teachers to send their classes to determine patterns of erosion; architectural drawing students to draft plans for renovation of historical buildings in the area—the type of service detailed in M. J. Cohen's futuristic *College of the Whole Earth* (1971) and in A. M. Cohen's "College of '79" (*Dateline '79* . . . 1969). The faculty members would have to recognize that these community-related activities are at least as useful as the textbook and lecture; would have to perceive them as the heart of the learning process, not as an adjunct. Above all, it would take a community-services director who could coordinate the activities so that they became a primary source of input to community problem-solving. Quite a job—but it will have to be done if community development is to supersede or even attain equal status with the instructional program.

The chance for such a merger appears slim. As with all questions in education the answers turn on the people involved. Colleges do not act; people do. Who will lead the colleges into the world of coordinated community development? The presidents and trustees stay busy keeping the institutions afloat. Faculty members are hurriedly banding together to preserve jobs and the status quo in instruction. The community-services director faces fellow second-echelon administrators who are concerned with their own programs, instructors whose perceived mission is to offer courses and advice only, and students whose primary concern is to accept what is offered.

Project Focus, a nationwide survey conducted by AACJC in 1971, provides corroboration. Presidents were asked how they rank the goals of the community college. The ninety respondents put the general goal, "Respond to needs of local community" fourth; but when it came to specific community-oriented goals, they invariably placed these near the bottom of the list (Bushnell, 1973, p. 50). For example, "Help solve social, economic, or political problems in the immediate geographical area," ranked twenty-third, and, "Help formulate programs in public policy areas, e.g., pollution control," twenty-fourth in a list of twenty-six (p. 55). The faculty members polled in the same survey responded similarly. They ranked "Respond to needs of local community" third but put the more specific community-service goal eleventh of twelve on their list (p. 51). And the students ranked the specific formulation of programs in public policy areas eleventh of twelve (p. 53). (At least the students were more consistent: they put the general statement "Respond to needs of local community" eighth in their listing.) To people within the colleges, community needs is apparently a nice thing to be committed to as long as it carries no commitment.

Within the college the community-service director is not in a position to influence policy through power or persuasion. His administrative colleagues typically fail to comprehend his broad aims, the instructors and counselors may ignore him totally, and the students are usually unaware of his existence. The college fiscal and personnel resources will not stretch to accommodate another function. The community he would serve is fractionated, with most of its elements anticipating at most traditional educative services for their tax dollars. And, unkindest cut of all, despite their calls for community development, his national spokesmen can offer examples of little more than uncoordinated program aggrandizement, tending in the main to ignore critical analysis, definitive objectives, and philosophical appraisal of what they are promoting.

Among the community presumably served, many people are dubious of what they perceive as noncollege functions. The uproar that results nearly every time colleges try closing for a teach-in on racism or war, or for electioneering, suggests a strong bias in favor of traditional teaching functions. Offering short courses off campus is fine, but meddling directly with social problems may be seen unkindly.

A major reason that the community development function has not reached parity with instruction—or even with student guidance—is that although its importance has been noted, the philosophical basis on which it stands has not been well articulated. When community development proponents state their case they conjure a group of people—an institution—immediately attentive to its constituency. Social theorists have long dreamed of the instantly responsive institution, the agency that stands ready to identify human needs and build a full complement of services to satisfy them. But to which needs should the institution respond and with what kinds of service?

"Good education" and "open recreational facilities" are universally appealing and uncompromisingly meaningless, for when goals are infinite, an unlimited number of forms may be built to contain them. If offering a course on the problems of aging at a local senior citizens' center is seen as equally valuable in enhancing the community as allowing neighborhood children to use the handball courts on campus after hours, what possibly could not fit the definition?

McClusky (1974) says that the community dimension means that *"all who desire and need to learn, whatever that learning may be"* are properly to be courted by the community college (p. 22). He refers to an inclusiveness of clientele that we are only beginning to comprehend: the disadvantaged, the rejects, the outsiders, as well as the well educated. Must we await a request for a course on safecracking, or firebomb-making, or modes of avoiding detection while shoplifting to realize the absurdity of that open-ended goal? Suppose our clientele want to learn how to write contracts with hard-to-detect loopholes. Suppose they want to learn the art of telling half-truths or of convincing people that they will deliver more than they actually expect to deliver. If the instruction to be offered to "all who desire and need to learn" is instruction defined in the college leaders' own terms with their own interpretation of socially desirable behavior, then the "community dimension" is based on dissimulation. If not, a crying need for more specific, finite goals is apparent.

The point is that the debate on community development has not been opened. How active should the college be? What percentage of its budget and staff time should be committed to community uplift? What will be accepted as evidence of program success? Most important, how far toward a role as welfare agency should the college go? Unasked by college spokesmen, these questions stand as silent testimony to educators' desires for institutional aggrandizement on the one hand and to their uncomprehension of educational philosophy on the other. They should at least be considered by those who, in their frenetic search for new clients, are attempting to propel the colleges into uncharted waters.

Despite proclamations of an intent to take over, the prognosis for an early flowering of the colleges as the national leaders for community-based education is not bright. For it is one thing to offer certain educational services as they have done, quite another to attempt to coordinate all services. University extension divisions and correspondence schools have offered community-based education for decades. So have the Boy Scouts, recreational departments, police and fire departments, Chambers of Commerce, auto clubs, insurance companies, and a host of others who may well take unkindly to being "coordinated" by self-appointed agents. Nor can the colleges slip easily into the spaces not presently filled by others, the areas that no one is serving. They are not uniquely endowed. As Lombardi

(1974) reminds us, "Probably, the most extravagant claim that can be made by some is that we must meet the community needs that are not served by any other agency. . . . There isn't any agency in the country that has been able to fulfill such a promise. There isn't a community college that has the resources to do so" (p. 8). To say that the community colleges will move into areas not now being served by other groups is to invite definition of a need—any need—in the program director's own terms. To say that they will coordinate all educational programs is to invite the charge, "Who sent for you?" from the directors of other, long-established agencies.

Looking ahead one can perceive jurisdictional controversy as the community colleges probe more vigorously into areas formerly accepted as the province of university extension, adult education divisions of public schools, and proprietary schools. Disputes will also arise between the colleges and welfare service agencies as the question of who gets money from what source becomes acute. But the basic issue determining how far the colleges go into community development is the extent to which their constituents feel they should be active agents.

Instructional services are passive. The client attends for his own reasons—to gain skill, enlightenment, certification, or merely because he has nothing more attractive to do. Trying to entice more people to submit to classes is considered fair practice. But the type of community service that reaches outside the classroom, depends on complex interagency arrangements, and duplicates services offered by other agencies is active. It is one thing to attempt to recruit students, quite another to become involved in welfare programs and competition with other agencies for social service dollars. Few constituents are ready for this stance on the part of the colleges. Few of the college personnel themselves are ready. And few of the advocates of community development recognize the difference between trying to entice students to enroll and trying to coordinate a variety of welfare service agencies. In brief, the colleges' "new mission" stands on an old, shaky base.

Chapter Eight

Experimental College Venture

A useful response to changing demands can be made within the college itself. Genuinely experimental programs have been introduced in several institutions. The idea of the experimental college is not new. Some of the oldest and most prestigious colleges and universities in America were conceived in response to demands for special educational institutions for special clienteles. Indeed, one might view the community college itself as a new type of institution and, thus, an experiment initiated to meet demands not satisfied by the more traditional schools.

Since the mid-1960s, however, there has been a new push toward experimental education. The so-called "free" schools at all levels are a response to dissatisfaction with typical educational offerings. Similarly, experimental colleges, schools-within-schools, colleges without walls, and even cluster colleges are reactions to students' cries for relevant education, parents' demands for more humane systems of education, and educators' desire to do a better job.

One reason experimental colleges have developed centers around the notion of postsecondary institutions as teaching institutions. Experimental colleges—at the two- or four-year college or university level—typically fail to include the elements of research and scholarship that pervade the broader university. Accordingly, the idea of the experimental college falls directly within the stated purposes of the two-year community college— to teach, rather than to conduct research. The experimental college thus extends the ideal of the community college by creating an environment where teaching can hold full sway.

Experimental colleges are instituted in answer to demands—often vociferous—by students, faculty, and taxpayers. But what specific purposes do these institutions serve? Are there pervasive themes that pertain to all forms of experimental programs?

Since the institutions of home and church, which have traditionally provided maturing experiences for youth, are diminishing in their effectiveness, colleges are becoming the social agencies that assume the task of bringing young people into society, of helping them to find their places, and of encouraging them to develop their own life styles. Perhaps more than other traditional institutions, experimental colleges strive toward this goal. Access to society is a major thrust of these programs, although that aim may be hidden.

Another way of viewing experimental colleges sees them as a safety valve for the traditional college that has failed to meet everyone's expectations. It is inevitable that an institution that promises to assist in the development of individual personality, to provide credentials for positions in the work force, to develop salable skills, to broaden intellectual and emotional horizons, to transmit culture and values, and to remedy educational defects occasioned by earlier schools that failed to live up to their promises, would disappoint at least some of its clients. Alternatives are needed to allay their frustrations. The experimental college promises to deliver at least part of that which larger, more comprehensive institutions cannot provide.

Most experimental colleges develop within larger institutions that are centered around residential clusters. They are built on new programs rather than on revisions of preexisting programs. The experimental college may offer a program for special students—the academically handicapped, the gifted, or those with particular interests—or it may have a more general appeal. Its purpose is described by Carpenter (1964), who notes that the experimental college "simply . . . is an educational institution which is trying to be a college. Literally a college is a community, a group of people [with] . . . varying ideas about what the community is trying to do. I should like to think that they are in pursuit of something more than surface phenomena, something more than imitation of other institutions. In trying to be a college, they have to ponder all of the factors which make this 'collegium' an especially valuable part of the larger needs of their clientele. . . . This will necessarily involve 'experimenting' " (pp. 1–2).

The experiments, of course, vary. While some experimental colleges offer traditional programs (for example, St. John's), most provide variations on the familiar themes. They are atypical. Antioch College may cease to be viewed as experimental because it has functioned consistently over many years, yet in its early days Antioch stood out as a unique conception of postsecondary education, focusing as it did on a work-study plan or cooperative program.

Stephens College, too, was considered unique in its beginnings and still has an experimental bent. Dedicated to a program that fosters the growth and development of each student in terms of individual interests as well as societal needs, it both provides a basic general education program and fosters experimentation in teaching (Leyden 1964). New College in Sarasota and Florida Presbyterian College are other examples of this type of experimental program, which may be found scattered throughout the country. These are all independent, single institutions; all were originally experimental in concept; and now all are prototypal.

Other experiments in postsecondary education are found in cluster colleges. California has several of these: the University of the Pacific in Stockton, the University of California at Santa Cruz, and the Claremont College complex—all of which have assumed a federated or cooperative approach. Fitting also into this category but acting as subcolleges rather than as independent but connected institutions are Monteith College, a development of Wayne State University (Michigan), and the General College of the University of Minnesota, which is unique because it initiated this variation. The federated approach—often adopted because it offers possible economies of scale and greater access to services—includes several independent but coalescent institutions, while the subcollege approach is dependent on the parent institution, even though the subcollege may have deviated greatly from the parent.

A variation is produced when a subcollege with close ties to its parent is formed. This subcollege might be portrayed more accurately as an experimental program—for example, Tussman's College at Berkeley, more formally known as the University of California Experimental College Program. This experiment was a short-lived response that grew out of the Free Speech Movement and its accordant demands for relevant educational experiences for undergraduate students. In a similar vein, Bensalem College was developed as a unit with special purposes in a larger institution (Fordham University, New York), as were the University of Massachusetts' two-year residential program, the University of Wisconsin's implementation of Meikeljohn's approach to education, San Francisco State Experimental College, and a host of other such outgrowths (see MacDonald, *Five Experimental Colleges,* 1973).

Lichtman (1971) fits all these programs into two categories: the innovative campus, which consists of a group of small, integrated, but semiautonomous colleges that are part of a large university system (for example, Santa Cruz); and the subcollege, which is located on the parent institution campus but is peripheral to its philosophy and programs (for instance, Bensalem). Several characteristics are held in common by these colleges, at least when they are initially projected (there is often a tendency to change in the course of implementation): the colleges are smaller than their parent organizations, the objective of smallness being the arousal of group loyalties; alternative liberal arts curriculums are offered; conventional disciplines are placed within the context of larger areas of knowledge, social problems, intellectual themes, or important figures; educational methods are flexible, encouraging such procedures as independent study, seminars, tutorials, student participation in governance, close student-faculty relations, and variations on the traditional academic calendar; often—almost always for four-year institutions—these colleges are residential, offering experiences in living and studying in the same area; a large amount of autonomy is generally given the experimental program by the sponsoring organization; and usually, these subgroups utilize the central administrative facilities of the parent institution.

Whatever the institutional organization, and however it attempts to deal with the varied forces impinging on it, several themes persist. Typically, these programs merge student counseling with instruction, thereby mitigating the separation that has arisen on most campuses between these two functions. Experimental colleges also frequently operate without grades or normative ranking of students. The curriculum of the experimental college is typically interdisciplinary, and student input into the curriculum plan is anticipated or actively encouraged. Some of these colleges attempt to provide off-campus learning experiences for their students, and contract learning or independent study is often a feature. Flexible timing or scheduling of classes is frequently seen. In nearly all cases, the intent is to bring a personal element to the campus by developing a sense of community among students and faculty who are involved in the experimental college. But whatever the intent, experimental colleges begin with high expectations for what they can accomplish.

Experimental colleges, although a longstanding element of postsecondary schooling, are less prevalent within the community colleges than in universities—perhaps in part because the community college may be viewed as an experiment in itself. The community college as a cluster of independent colleges is especially rare, probably because the idea of the cluster college differs little from the idealized version of the small college that sequesters itself from the broader community—a mode of operation that is antithetical to the community college ethos. Indeed, although a few two-year colleges have tried the cluster college organization, results have been mixed. For example, the

College of DuPage (Illinois) has devised a cluster college mode, but it is not clearly defined. Certain faculty are identified as being members of each cluster, but the student body in each is an amorphous group who may or may not be taking all or most of their courses within the cluster. Nor has the autonomy and responsibility for each cluster been clearly defined as it relates either to other clusters or to the central administration.

Student-run colleges as adjuncts to two-year colleges are even more rare than subcolleges and cluster colleges. This is understandable because the short time that students are involved with two-year colleges and the nonresidential character of most of these institutions mitigate the coalescence of a group of like-minded people determined to pursue their own education in their own way. In four-year institutions where these colleges have developed, students have assumed responsibility for defining the curriculum, employing staff, and making all administrative decisions. From an educational standpoint, these are high-risk ventures.

An experimental college that has developed apparently successfully within the community college format is one in which the entire institution operates quite differently from other two-year colleges. This somewhat rare category usually addresses itself to special educational problems—attrition, personal and vocational guidance, and the like. La Guardia Community College of CUNY, for example, is designed to offer a five-year educational program to underachieving students from the tenth grade through the community college. Basic skills training is provided in the context of career exploration, along with an interdisciplinary curriculum. The La Guardia College plan includes cooperative work education with the goal that all students will be placed in jobs by the conclusion of their second year of affiliation with the institution. In effect, it has accepted responsibility for basic education and for ameliorating the dropout problem in the formal school system, and it represents, accordingly, a test of the mass higher education construct.

However, an entire college organized as an experimental college is unusual. More prevalent is the experimental program —less a separate college or division than a special group of staff members who, with administrative sanction, devise a sequence of courses and other experiences for special students. The "exploratory year" at Greenfield Community College (Massachusetts)—a model program of occupational exploration for students who are uncertain about their vocational goals— fits this category and provides the introduction to an in-depth analysis of a program of this type.

Greenfield's exploratory year began in spring 1972, enrolling twenty-six first-semester freshmen who were unsure of their future career plans. These students enrolled in four introductory courses: English, psychology, speech, and the sociology of work. The sociology course, which was the core of the program, was designed to create a situation in which participants could comfortably merge hard career data with significant lifestyle choices. This course had four components: classroom study of the sociology of work; a ten-week independent study of some aspect of the sociology of work; eight minicourses presenting data about various life-style choices (the student was required to attend at least three); and a two-to-three-week work placement during which no other courses were taken. Participants generally felt that the program was valuable: twenty-four of the twenty-six students were successfully helped in firming their occupational plans. Despite the fact that the number of students involved in the experimental group was small, on the basis of these results the program was adopted as part of the regular school curriculum for the 1973–1974 school year.

What are the forces that lead up to developing an experimental college as a program within an existing college? What makes an experimental program viable? Why are so many dropped after a year or so while others remain somewhat intact or are incorporated into the regular college program? By way of answering these questions, we present an assessment of an experimental program that was developed within a comprehensive community college (for a full report, see Cohen and Brawer, 1974).

Rio Hondo College (California) is a comprehensive community college. The idea for the Exploratory College—a college within a college—was bruited by several department chairmen,

administrators, faculty representatives, and members of the
board of trustees, who perceived the need for Rio Hondo College to redefine general education experiences for students, to
provide options to the regular curriculum and instructional
forms, and to assist students in determining their academic and
career goals. All were considered within the broader framework
of providing better educational opportunities at the college in
order to mollify student disaffection and to attract more students from population segments that were not attending the
college in large numbers.

As the plan evolved, the notion of an exploratory college
emerged. This would be a place where students could learn
in an unpressured environment, sort out their academic and
career goals, "perhaps waste a year," as one board member put
it. Short courses, curriculum sampling without penalty, informal teaching, and an enthusiastic staff would meliorate student
dropout. The idea of the community as a learning resource was
also noted. In addition, the Exploratory College would serve as
an outlet for the creative impulses of some of the faculty and
would be a source of ideas that would eventually change the
rest of the college, which otherwise was crystallizing. The college was not to be an elitist or separate operation but was to
serve as a holding station for students pending their melding
into the regular programs. The staged aspect of the college
would see students attending for from two or three weeks to a
year.

These general intentions to do something about student
dissatisfaction, faculty creative impulses, a congealing college
program, and student guidance predictably led to a variety of
perceptions as to what the college was supposed to be. According to the faculty of the college at large, the Exploratory College was instituted as a place to help students define their vocational goals, learn more about career alternatives, define their
academic goals, and develop better study habits. However, the
faculty actually involved with the Exploratory College was not
as uniformly positive about this guidance function, feeling that
the College should help students to define vocational goals and

learn more about career alternatives, but, in addition, should encourage academic independence and help students participate in community services.

A second major function of the college was as a place where different instructional techniques and curriculum patterns could be tried out. This would allow faculty members a chance to experiment. Presumably, it would also eventually encourage change in the regular college programs.

The Exploratory College was launched in 1972. It quickly attracted the seekers, those students who desired something different because they were not clear as to what they wanted for a career or an academic major or because they sought experience different from that which could be obtained in the regular college program. As seen by the Exploratory College faculty, students in this program were more motivated, interesting, creative, and community-minded, and less goal-directed than the students in the regular college. As seen by the regular college staff, they were more interesting and creative and less motivated, goal-directed, community-minded, studious, and mature. The discrepancies in perceptions are noteworthy.

The staff for the Exploratory College were recruited from the regular college faculty by the simple expedient of the director going to each department, describing the program, and asking for volunteers. Six faculty members (in addition to the director) became involved with the Exploratory College in its first year. Eventually there were as many as ten members.

The faculty stated they were attracted by the chance to work in a relaxed atmosphere with small student groups. They wanted the opportunity for flexible scheduling, the chance to build interdisciplinary courses, the option to abandon punitive grade marking, to interact with students directly, to develop friendships, and to operate closely with other people (the need for community is no less with faculty than with students). In general, they sought collegiality, informality, and a minimum of bureaucracy, and they reacted against the paraphernalia of grades, prerequisites, time blocks and scheduling, and the requirements that have grown up around all colleges.

The faculty modified several aspects of the original plan

for the College. The fact that they had a predominantly liberal arts focus shaped the curriculum, intentionally or not, and the fact that they saw the most important function of the Exploratory College as helping students gain personal development led them to minimize career exploration and vocational guidance.

Accordingly, the College developed along the lines of staff members' predilections; however, this should not be viewed as an untoward consequence. The College was to be a place where people could try out different techniques, do things in their own way without the pressures of scheduling and particularized course and program requirements. It is understandable, then, that with this open charter the College took the form assigned by its faculty. One board member expressed unease by saying, "I wish we had some objectives, a plan for accomplishment. The board should have held them to specifics," but he recognized that the Exploratory College had been given what amounted to a blank check.

The effects of the Exploratory College can be related to the perceptions of the students and staff members—those within the Exploratory College and in the broader college community. Because few specific objectives were set, little hard data are available. One general effect must be noted early on: the basic promise of the Exploratory College that it would be a place where some faculty and students could work out their version of an educational program with an absolute minimum of interference from the outside—a goal they achieved beyond doubt.

Perhaps most important (and consistent with Jencks and others', 1972, thesis that schools should be happy places in which to function), an overwhelming majority of students stated that they enjoyed their experiences in the Exploratory College. Students also agreed that their experiences there helped them to become more self-directed, even though few of them felt that they had had sufficient direction toward a realistic assessment of their abilities. Apparently the pattern of experiences in the Exploratory College led the students to believe that they were gaining self-direction even though the direction from the staff did not lead them toward self-assessment. Thus the main effect of encouraging students to be more self-directed was pursued.

The interdisciplinary nature of Exploratory College offerings was also appreciated by the students, most of whom said they were assisted in recognizing the interrelatedness of different subject areas. This basic general education function was, then, effected. However, fewer than half the students claimed they were able to relate their experiences in the Exploratory College to the district community. Hence, this broader aspect of general education was fulfilled to a much lesser degree.

Despite general appreciation of the program on the part of involved students, the Exploratory College has been consistent with regular two-year programs in its difficulty in holding students. Enrollments fell off slightly from the high of 154 in the first semester (fall 1972) to 140 in spring 1974. More relevant than the actual figures, however, is the fact that it took augmented publicity efforts to maintain these numbers.

As for effects on the faculty, an overwhelming majority of staff members who were not involved with the program said it had no effect on them. This is quite revealing for what it says about the program aim of feeding ideas back to the rest of the campus. Undoubtedly an experimental program affects those who are involved in it more intensely than it does those who have had no experience with it.

Curriculum and instruction are at the heart of any educational enterprise. So it was with the Exploratory College. More concern and effort were expended on curriculum and instruction than on any other aspect of the College (such as facilities, materials, staffing, student selection). The curriculum was to be centered on the humanities with four outcomes intended: career exploration, student self-knowledge, interrelation of all subjects, and knowledge of community and society. In short, this was to be an integrated general education sequence. And the faculty who were attracted to the Exploratory College originally felt it would allow them to build integrated courses in which they could relate their own disciplines to those of other instructors at the College. At the same time, from its inception, the Exploratory College curriculum was strongly committed to integrate academic guidance and career exploration.

The idea that the Exploratory College would be built on a minimum of competition for grade marks was established early, along with the aforementioned informal atmosphere. Nonpunitive grade marking (the abolition of Ds and Fs) was seen as an idea whose time had arrived.

The intent to build minicourses and to develop modular scheduling was more successful than were efforts to assist students in making career choices—most of the first-year students felt they were able to function comfortably within the flexible scheduling arrangement. However, flexible scheduling caused problems because classes overlapped with each other and with those in the regular program. And although the faculty generally approved of the modules, some felt that a sense of community among Exploratory College students and faculty members was lost when there was no class that everyone attended at the same time.

Similarly, the informality in classroom arrangement had widespread appeal. Students reported they felt more involved with their fellows and with their instructors in the informal arrangements, and faculty members who taught in these circumstances seemed to enjoy them as well. However, a few of the regular college staff expressed extreme displeasure at the spectacle of barefooted students sitting on pillows in class. Obviously there is a definite line between instructors and students who like to work in traditional, formal classrooms, where the patterns of interaction are more apparently structured, and those who like the sense of freedom obtained in the informal classroom. Sizable numbers of both students and faculty feel more comfortable in one situation than in the other.

The Rio Hondo Exploratory College was planned at a time when many students and faculty on every campus were articulating vigorously the need for a place for dialogue, a "relevant" environment, one that would satisfy their desire for immediate conversation, good feelings, and "vibes." Although

Rio Hondo College was not afflicted with an excess of this verbalized dissatisfaction with traditional educational forms, the demand for alternatives was reflected in the Exploratory College plans and procedures. The College projected an image of freedom from authority and responsibility.

Whether at the two- or four-year college or university level, there are persistent themes in the development of experimental colleges, just as there are persistent results. First and foremost, experimental colleges tend to have a short life span. Students' enthusiasm wanes rapidly as they realize that the college does not—perhaps cannot—fulfill their expectations. Resources dry up when the supporting agent—whether an administrator, a college governing board, or an extramural funding agency loses interest in the experiment. Faculty turnover is high; the failure of expectation afflicts instructors as well as students. In short, centrifugal force characterizes the interaction among faculty, students, and supporting agents initially attracted by the grandiose claims of the founders.

Another phenomenon of most experimental colleges is that whether they originally intend to serve a broad spectrum of students, or whether they are set up for specialized groups, certain students tend to cluster around them unless matriculation is strictly regulated. Students who are typically attracted to experimental colleges are reported as being self-centered, curious, creative, verbose, and utopian. They are rarely a cross-section of those who attend the institution at large. And as a result, a particular type of program develops.

Also notable is that the rank and file of faculty in the regular college program object to the experiment. Some feel threatened by a group that has attained special support for engaging in its own preferred instruction, and they fail to understand the intent of the experiment—either through inadequate description on the part of the college planners or because they do not want to understand. Some feel the broader institution is compromised by having a separate group within it, particularly because the goals of the experimental college are frequently much like an elaborate restatement of the goals of the broader institution. Other faculty members wish to maintain an authority relationship with their students that is diminished in an experimental college.

For the faculty within the experimental college there are other problems. These instructors join the experiment because they are dissatisfied with the traditional pattern of rigid curriculum, fixed hours, grade marking, prerequisites, and other accouterments of college teaching. They may be unclear as to viable options to these patterns, but they do feel that anything different is worth trying. However, as they become involved with the experimental college and undertake student counseling along with a fair portion of the administration of the subunit, they find their work day lengthened markedly. Fatigue and consequent disaffection afflicts them after a year or two.

Any assessment of the effects of experimental colleges in American higher education is difficult to verify because of the Hawthorne Effect. Many of the claims to success must be weighed against the fact that experimental colleges are almost invariably new—most fail within three years unless they are substantially modified. Of the experimental ventures that have survived longer, most have done so by compromising their original principles; in order to avoid the charge of elitism or favoritism and in order to maintain their enrollment they have broadened their offerings so that they have become barely distinguishable from the parent college. Here one can say that the institution itself has so co-opted the experiment, that although it may survive, it really survives in name only.

When it comes to the community college, the experimental college within the institution faces a difficult future. Certain features of successful experimental colleges cannot easily be duplicated in the two-year community college. The residential or student cluster pattern fosters a sense of community that is difficult to achieve in a commuter institution, where the college is only one of many influences on the students' outlook and where faculty and students have little more in common than their dissatisfaction with traditional education. Because faculty and students lack common interests, backgrounds, and goals, cooperation in planning and conduct of the educational program is not easy. The high expectations and inflated claims with which experimental colleges are launched also tend to lead quickly to disenchantment.

Nevertheless, the experimental college seems to have a place within the community college because it does promise to develop a feeling of community within what have become generally large, amorphous institutions. Experimental colleges provide a place where dissident faculty feel they are in control of their own instructional processes and where certain students feel they are particularly welcome. As such, the experimental college within the community college acts as a safety valve for pressures that might otherwise be vented in less productive arenas. For the institution this is rather like the person who has money in the bank "for a rainy day": it is nice to think and talk about it even if one never has to use it.

A shortcoming of many ventures in education is that the planners feel they must promise to solve, or at least mitigate, numerous problems in order to gain initial approval and continued support for their project. These promises are made so that competing ventures can be superseded or so that various groups represented by members of the planning committee can be satisfied. Subsequently, disillusionment sets in when the supporting agencies or the client populations realize that most of the problems the project promised to solve are still present. The experimental program may be successful in a few of the intended activities, but one program cannot do everything, no matter how well planned, staffed, and supported.

Given the obvious inability of one person or one institution to satisfy all demands, could experimental colleges still make more lasting impressions on their students, faculties, and postsecondary education itself? A number of ways to achieve this might be suggested. For example, it would be possible to place sizable numbers of students into an experimental program merely by making that experience mandatory for all who fail to declare their major upon matriculation. This alternative would demand a focus on assisting students in making academic and career choices and a concomitant turn away from the emphasis on informality for all.

An experimental program could be established as a sub-college where ideas are tried out and then incorporated into the regular program, but it would be successful only if a number of different instructors were involved, working out their own ideas and then bringing them back to their own classes. This suggests frequent changes in staff so that more instructors would be involved for shorter periods of time. A "sabbatical-in-instruction-in-residence" plan could be tried, which would enable instructors to take a semester or a year in the experimental program with the understanding that they would introduce their own forms of instruction. This would have the effect of maximizing the experimental college function as a disseminator of ideas, but it would be difficult to maintain a core program or guiding ethos to serve students. To work well this type of college would have to be nearly totally labile in its curriculum and instructional forms. Nevertheless it would satisfy the problem of maintaining faculty enthusiasm.

Even when college boards and administrative staffs are committed to the idea of an experimental program, other forces tend to reduce general faculty support for new ventures. Primary is the faculty fear of being left out on a limb with a new program when layoffs are threatened because of general enrollment declines. The traditional departments seem safer to them in the face of this development. Unless definite commitments are made to retain faculty members even if the experiment fails, new staff may be less than willing to commit themselves.

A commitment to experimentation might be resolved by setting forth a plan for several experimental programs, each with its own budget and guarantees of staff reemployment. Or a ten-year plan for successive experimental colleges could be adopted, to be organized first around one theme, then another, showing that the commitment to experimentation would continue regardless of the success of any one venture. Some action of this type will be necessary if an experimental program demanding a sizable commitment on the part of an individual faculty member is to continue to attract candidates.

The idea of an experimental college as a continuing renewal area is certainly commendable, but certain caveats must be observed. If the intent is to establish an open-ended experimental program where people can try various educational forms without precise goals, there must be a strict pattern of faculty and student recruitment and selection. Failing this, homogeneity is inevitable, because like-minded staff and students will cluster and work out a program that seems best to them, leading others to perceive a parochial operation and consequently to refuse to lend support.

Voluntary enrollment on the part of students and staff can be maintained, however, if the planning group defines precise objectives, accountability measures, and time constraints. Under this design the faculty who participate understand exactly what goals they are required to fulfill and set their programs accordingly. However, time and funds for deliberate staff training must be provided. It is not enough to allow the staff released time to grope in the general problem area; an expert in the field of concern must design and implement a staff training program. The board and the administration can hold them responsible for their effects. Understandably, quite a different type of faculty member and student is attracted to a program with clearly defined goals to which they understand they are expected to adhere. Nevertheless such a plan might well be considered as a type of experimental college.

One alternative approach might well be a carefully designed experiment in curriculum and instruction with its own clearly articulated instructional objectives and its own processes of collecting data on the effect it has on students and staff members. This would mean an exploratory or experimental college that would establish a liaison with an instructional research office to get aid with the construction of objectives and data collection and analytic procedures. Pre- and post-testing, student follow-up, and carefully controlled curriculum and instructional treatments would be part of such an enterprise. Also a part would be the continuing publication of effects so that the college and the community could be kept apprised of outcomes. The director of such an experimental program should be conversant with the concept of defined outcomes, believe in the utility of the concept, and be able to assist other staff members in translating their own ideas into this language.

Another experimental approach might develop programs around disciplinary areas, a pattern similar to the cluster college or house plan, in which students and staff members who are interested in studying health sciences or liberal arts or social sciences work together in their own area. Such a program is most suitable for the diffusion of ideas into the regular departments because it is in fact constructed and maintained by people from common curriculum areas. It seems not exceptionally well suited to the community college because so few of the entering students are certain of their curriculum interests and because they drop in and out repeatedly, thus mitigating program continuity. However, Cypress College (California) has operated a house plan successfully since 1967.

An experimental program in career exploration could be built, centered neither on vocational-technical training, the humanities, nor any other discipline. Instead, it would teach students about the work world—what it means to be a citizen functioning in an industrial or a postindustrial society. Its curriculum and instructional forms would emphasize how one maintains oneself and how this relates to one's own personal preferences. It would include elements of the relationship of humanistic thought to work as well as discussions and examples of art in the work place. Demonstrations, simulated performance, and actual practice would be part of the instructional plan. Students and staff members would be screened for entry to the program; it could not be operated on a voluntary enrollment procedure.

If occupations are to be stressed, a program that puts together students and faculty to design the continually needed new occupational curriculums could be built. Here would be a corps of staff and apprentices working with off-campus enterprises to determine new training needs and to set up the programs—off campus if necessary. This community-involvement occupational program would have the students learn about different occupations not only by studying or working in them, but also by designing the programs necessary to train other people to work in them. Students thus involved in curriculum design would actually be learning an occupation at the highest level. This program would also be useful in gaining public support for the college as the occupational curriculum design teams worked with business and industrial groups in helping them to devise their own training programs.

Yet another form of experimentation might be a program organized on modular current-interest courses. Here the students would not enroll in the experimental college as such. Instead the program would arrange short courses, intensive lecture series, and other self-contained events. Students from the regular programs would be encouraged to participate in these minicourses rather than to become experimental college students. This pattern would have the major distinction of being a "disposable" curriculum, with short courses standing or falling on their own merits. A joint student-faculty committee could operate it, defining areas of current interest and arranging short courses. The program would allow for intensive study in certain fields for certain students, shifting from women's studies to programs for the aged to any number of other specialized areas. Some juggling in registration and course crediting procedures would be necessary so that students could get fractional credit. This program would allow students to gain credit just for the time they are in attendance and let them drop in and out of the college without penalty and without the necessity of advance enrollment.

These are but a few of the ideas for alternative experimental colleges. The desirability of one or another experimental form could be explored with the admonition that no program can satisfy a plethora of disparate aims. Genuine experimental programs have a place in two-year colleges. They require thought, commitment, and evaluation and should not be treated as an easy way of pacifying vociferous students and faculty members. Indeed, they may give us more than we ask for.

Chapter Nine

Understanding the Faculty

All the waves of demands for staff members who are sympathetic to "new" students and who can take colleges toward their new ports splash against the current faculty. Most of these people were employed when the primary function of colleges was teaching, not welfare or community development. They enlisted in the institutions with that function in mind and adopted a commensurate role. They are there and will be there for a generation at least, and they cannot be ignored.

Although this point seems self-evident, most research studies and reports that describe the problems of designing and implementing suitable programs fail to take account of it. The faculty is recognized as having primary responsibility for effecting student learning, but only rarely are attempts made to tie institutional processes back to faculty functioning. Instead, governance structures, finances, administrative policies, and statewide coordination are seen as the keys to curriculum and instructional forms. The same holds true when different higher education institutions are compared. They are usually identified by their location; their classification as private or public, college or university; their physical features; and the students enrolled.

Little is reported about faculty characteristics or effectiveness.

Accordingly we have only minimal information about faculty. This meager information base applies in particular to community college instructors. Although at least two books (Cohen and Brawer, 1972; Kelley and Wilbur, 1970) are devoted to this group, most reports are either parochial or are included in works on instructors at other types of colleges and universities. And while "descriptive studies of college and university faculty are neither new nor uncommon, . . . typically the comprehensiveness and diversity of the information collected [are] inversely related to the sample size" (Bayer, 1970, p. 1).

Approximately 140,000 people teach in public and private junior/community colleges. Understandably there is no single approach to describing them; psychological and sociological approaches have been used. In other words, variables borrowed from several social sciences are applied whenever data on faculty are collected. Frequently the populations studied are chosen for convenience only; a graduate student in sociology or psychology who happens at the same time to be an instructor in a two-year college surveys his or her colleagues, plugs the data into a theory associated with the parent discipline, and reports on the validity of the theory. The studies are almost never repeated by using the same theory on a comparable data pool or the same data in support of a different theory.

The psychological and sociological research on college faculty—covering general characteristics, types, selection, and training—is summarized by Brawer (1968), who, taking an eclectic view, suggests that no one type of person can be called an instructor, no one way can be followed for selecting a faculty member, and no one approach can be used for understanding him or her. Personality characteristics are also considered in an evaluation by Cohen and Brawer (1969) which presents reasons for using student achievement of learning objectives as the main basis for studies of faculty and of instructional effect and gives designs for assessing instructors.

Psychological theory forms the basis of one book on two-year college instructors: Cohen and Brawer (1972) make a plea for faculty maturity through personal identity and self-awareness—a sense of directedness toward professional development. They comment on the way the mature instructor arranges procedures "so that he tends to judge himself—and to be judged— by his effects. Whatever role he plays—model, mediator, or instructional manager—he must be his own mentor. He adopts particular functions because they suit his personality and the needs of the institution and people he serves. He adjusts his activities to his effects on his students. He becomes a professional instructor—one who causes learning" (p. 221).

When researchers working in the field of education— usually students or professors affiliated with a graduate program or institutional researchers—set out to determine the characteristics of a faculty, they usually apply no theory at all. Demographic variables dominate; we know much about the men and women on the faculty in individual colleges: number, age, ethnicity, number of siblings and progeny, and educational level of parents. But unless studies of faculty are tied to theories of human functioning, they lack comparability, and their ability to supply explanations is negligible. Raw data pools do have a use but only when the data are collected in a uniform manner over a period of years. Most single-college studies are one-shot affairs.

Most studies are compilations of actuarial or demographic data. Medsker and Tillery (1971), for example, report findings from a survey of four thousand instructors taken from a stratified sample of fifty-seven community colleges throughout the country. They note that: community college staffs are composed primarily of people in the thirty-one-to-fifty-year-old bracket; the master's degree is the highest degree held by most instructors; staff members are recruited from a wide variety of sources, with almost 33⅓ percent of the respondents coming from the public school system, 22 percent directly from graduate school, 11 percent from positions in four-year institutions, 10 percent from business and industry, and the remainder from various other sources; few junior college faculty members are from minority groups; and "the social class background of many white staff members makes it difficult for them to relate to students from various ethnic groups" (p. 90). These data were derived from an early survey, and some changes might better reflect conditions in the 1970s, especially in regard to the conclusion about selection and recruitment, but the last point demands special consideration in light of current demands that faculty be seen as relevant and sympathetic to their students.

These studies, whether psychological, sociological, or demographic, provide information about instructors as a single group. Other investigations distinguish classes of instructors. For instance, Eckert and Williams (1972) studied 1383 instructors from forty-three colleges and universities in Minnesota and compared data for the various institutions. Four-year public institution instructors were primarily male, born out of state, PhDs, and most concerned with their research opportunities. Four-year private institution instructors were mostly male, born out of state, PhDs, and greatly concerned with their relationships with colleagues. Public junior college instructors were mainly male, born in the state, MAs, and most concerned with the age and type of students they taught. And private junior college instructors were primarily female, born in the state, MAs, and most concerned with the kinds of student they dealt with. The American Council on Education also surveys college and university faculties, but these studies are broad in scope and are more statistical than interpretative (Bayer, 1970; 1973). Yet another look at faculties in various institutions was undertaken by the Berkeley Center for Research and Development in Higher Education, which sampled 1069 subjects representing six schools in three states (Wilson and Gaff, 1969). These included a large public university, a small and a medium-sized private university, a large state college, a medium-sized public junior college, and a small private liberal arts college. Noteworthy in that it presents a view of faculty based on ideological grounds rather than demographic or personality characteristics, this study assessed opinions regarding student participation in campus governance. Of interest, too, is Morey's (1972) review of 106 documents pertaining to traits, preparation, and evaluation of community college faculty, who must contend with a wide diversity of students; professional isolation from the "community of scholars"; a teaching schedule that may include several areas of specialization, and teaching loads from fifteen to eighteen hours per week; nonteaching assignments, such as academic advisement, counseling, supervision of student activities, and committee memberships; and a median salary of $10,850, with salary schedules based on experience and length of service.

Faculty are becoming more diverse. Increasingly, they are being recruited from graduate schools, industry, the professions, and four-year colleges, rather than from high schools, as they were in the 1960s. Gleazer (1967), Kelly and Connolly (1970), and Siehr (1963) suggest a trend toward hiring instructors who have a master's degree and a diversity in personal characteristics, academic preparation, and previous job experience. As a result faculty frequently disagree with the stated purposes of their colleges, and demographic and educational differences are reflected among teachers according to their high or low acceptance of the goals of their institutions. At the same time, most faculty agree that their most important work-related problems are difficulty in motivating students, lack of professional refreshment, and unfamiliarity with transfer requirements.

Project Focus provides information about faculty, students, and presidents. From a sampling of 2491 faculty members, Bushnell (1973) reports a high degree of agreement between the rank-ordering of the same goals by both presidents and faculty. Points of consensus include "serving the higher educational needs of youth from the surrounding community, helping students develop a respect for their own abilities and an understanding of their limitations, responding to the needs of the local community, and helping students acquire the ability to adapt to new occupational requirements as technology and society change. . . . [However, while presidents] tend to emphasize responding to community needs more strongly . . . faculty place greater stress on the students' personal development" (p. 48). Despite such evinced dedication to personal development in their students, faculty continue to use a double standard—not always feeling that students should share an equal voice on policy matters—and both faculty and student groups feel they are not sufficiently involved in decision-making.

Patterson (1971) says that a clearer understanding of attitudes of faculty with various career experiences is needed if community colleges are to be successful in helping faculty put their objectives, philosophies, and programs into practice. In order to gain such understanding, Pennsylvania college faculty were studied to determine the relationship between previous career experiences and attitudes toward educational issues. Faculty who had not held previous assignments were more progressive than faculty who had worked in a public school, a junior college, a four-year college, business or industry, or another area. The "progressive respondents," in improving their own approaches to instruction, may be the prime movers toward the achievement of institutional goals, a statement consistent with that of Williams (1970), who reports that faculty members who have opportunities to be involved in policy formulation are in the process of changing from their own traditional roles of noninvolvement to a more active participation in school governance.

Freedman and Bloom (1973), report certain significant subgroup differences—between scientists and humanists, researchers and teachers, and cosmopolitan and local faculty. Comparing attitudes of junior college instructors, Medsker and Tillery (1971) note that 43 percent oriented themselves toward the senior college. They supported the liberal arts aspects of the junior college while rejecting its comprehensive functions. Those who had never attended a junior college and who taught in an applied area, rejected three of five functions descriptive of the junior college, including remedial and community services functions; felt admission requirements should not be different for different students; and rejected vocational work for adults.

Studies of faculties in single schools and studies of instructors in a number of institutions provide base lines from which to ask further questions, just as do investigations comparing respondents from various institutions—two-year colleges, four-year liberal arts colleges, and multiuniversities. The singular studies are, by definition, parochial, although they often provide insight into a college staff that is not otherwise available. And, once completed, these studies may be compared like the multiinstitutional investigations, which, while employing better methodology and stimulating more data, lump faculties together, thereby neutralizing their findings.

According to Martin's report (1969) on 577 faculty members from eight apparently diverse schools, cross-cuts on data, "whether by age categories, publications, academic specializations, teaching load; whether old or new schools, conventional or innovative, show that faculty are more alike than dissimilar in their attitudes toward educational assumptions, values, and goals; the criteria for institutional excellence; and the prospects for professional or institutional change. . . . On item after item there were no statistically significant differences among faculty, while comparative data analyses made clear their overwhelming degree of like-mindedness. Differences that appeared were often a matter of degree" (p. 206). If Martin's information discloses such homogeneity among faculties in schools that had been selected initially because of their apparent diversity, can we expect diversity among a smaller number of instructors?

Using three comprehensive community colleges (Urban, Suburban, and Rural) located within one hundred miles of Los Angeles, we will compare faculty to determine what differences exist between colleges and what influence each college has on its instructors. If we find that differences are greater than similarities among instructors, then it follows that in-service programs must be individually tailored. But if there is a similarity or homogeneity among the faculty members in the seemingly different schools, then the same models or programs to increase faculty development may well apply to all the institutions.

Urban College, established in 1927, is a large community college in an urban-industrial area of some 250,000 people, and has six feeder high schools. It has a total faculty of 186, 97 of whom are part-time, and approximately 1600 full-time and 1100 part-time students.

Urban College was once a "rah-rah" school, which boasted a nationally recognized football team. With pride in the number of its graduates who went on to four-year colleges and

universities, it was respected by its supporting community; as
an institution that represented primarily a white, middle-class
population, it acted as an agent of upward mobility. Going to
college meant a step up the ladder for many of its students and,
less direct but perhaps as important, for their parents.

Along with its supporting community, Urban College
has undergone several changes during the years—a decline in
athletic dominance and a change in its ethnic composition. Now
that postsecondary schooling is more expected than unique,
when enrollments in most institutions of higher learning are
markedly increased from the 1920s, Urban College has fewer students in relation to its district population. Because of lowered
enrollment, few new faculty members are employed, and those
instructors who have been at Urban College for a decade or
more have seen the character of their school change markedly.
Whereas in the 1930s many students transferred to universities
from this community college, only about 340 now obtain an
AA degree annually, and fewer than 500 go on to further
schooling—at least immediately after securing the associate degree or sufficient credits to transfer. Pride in the football team,
in the school publications, and in other such activities, has dis-
sipated.

Suburban College is in many ways the antithesis of the
inner-city school. The junior member of a two-campus district,
it serves an area of 361,000 people, has eight high schools feeding into it, and employs 128 faculty members, only 6 of whom
are part-time. The area surrounding Suburban College is composed of predominantly white, conservative, middle- and upper-
middle-class families, the majority of whom commute to work
in other areas.

Perhaps more than most community colleges, this campus
has a certain amount of latitude to develop an educational program for the needs of its students and its community in general. Because of limited facilities it concentrated in its early
years on courses and curriculums that did not require extensive
and expensive facilities and equipment, and it encouraged its
instructors to design their own equipment. Originally, in fact,

a number of Suburban College faculty members were recruited from the older college because they wanted to innovate.

Seventy-five percent of Suburban College students indicate that they want to transfer, but only about 25 percent actually do so; 5 percent become occupational majors, and 70 percent are neither transfer nor occupational students. This picture of transfer selection mirrors many other institutions and is matched by a representative attrition rate. However, one of the greatest differences between this institution and other colleges is that it does not seem to be an agent of upward mobility for its community. Whereas many students in community colleges are the first in their families to attend college, a large proportion of Suburban students have parents who hold college degrees. Thus, rather than serving as a step in upward mobility, Suburban College maintains the status quo by enrolling students who often do not care about further schooling, but who enroll because of parental expectation.

Rural College, notably different from the other two institutions in our study, is a two-year college in a rural community that covers 2500 square miles but numbers only 60,000 people. Fairly new, its relatively few students are typically drawn from four feeder high schools. It has sixty-five faculty members, thirty-seven full-time and twenty-eight part-time.

The Rural College administration encourages the development of multimedia instructional programs, enabling students to learn at their own rate and providing staff members an opportunity to use their innovative abilities. In both quantity and quality of equipment and materials, Rural College ranks among the best in the state.

Whereas Urban College is potentially an agent of upward mobility and Suburban College acts as a control on downward mobility, this school functions more as a self-contained institution. Approximately 40 percent of its 1300 students continue their education in four-year colleges and universities, and, since few of their parents have had college experience, this institution acts as a springboard for socioeconomic movement upward and outward, away from the home town. Those who don't transfer stay in their isolated area and farm, pump gas, wait tables, work at the local air base. The college just sits out there in a big open field. For some students, it's a step on the way out. For most it's just a few months of high school postgraduate study.

The following data were obtained from a 1969 survey of faculty and administrative staffs at each of the three subject colleges. From their responses the subjects are described in terms of selected demographic variables, college affiliation, and values, as obtained from Rokeach's Instrumental and Terminal Values Scales.

Sixty-five respondents to the staff survey reported holding the AA, suggesting that about 27 percent of the total surveyed have attended a junior college. In addition, 221 hold BAs, 184 hold MAs; 36 are designated "other." Urban College has 22 faculty and staff members holding the AA degree, 76 the BA, 60 the MA, and 7 "others." The Suburban College staff hold 36 AAs, 113 BAs, 95 MAs, and 10 "others." The notably smaller staff in the Rural College reported that 7 instructors have attained the AA degree; 32 the BA, 29 the MA, and 7 "others." Most degrees were obtained in a public four-year college or university, although some faculty designated denominational schools, private colleges, or teacher's colleges as their degree-granting institutions. As the figures suggest, the faculties from all three schools are substantially the same in their educational backgrounds.

Some other findings are noteworthy. Half the faculty respondents favor the lecture method, despite the fact that two colleges consider themselves innovative. A real disparity is evident in terms of the grading system desired—although most instructors chose a pass-fail system, 97 of the 238 respondents still preferred the security of the letter grade.

When it comes to what they think students want in teaching, most faculty members indicated that students would like "interesting lectures." However, as Cohen reports (1970), while all three faculties ranked "Specify learning objectives" last or next to last, entering freshmen responding to a similar instrument ranked this item first. "Further, when each instructor was asked what he thought his students would like him to do, 'Specify learning objectives for them' was marked by two-thirds of the group. Thus, a majority of instructors felt their students would *like* objectives specified for them. At the same time they thought objectives were the *last* things students look for" (p. 58). It is always difficult for one person to get into the mind of another, but the contradiction here is especially noteworthy. Most instructors still refuse to believe that students want to know what is expected of them, want to be given a frame on which they can hang what they hear in the classroom and read in their books. Specific objectives serve that purpose.

Other differences between students and staff, which in some cases point to a strong argument for irreconcilability between the groups, are explored in a study of student and staff values (Brawer, 1971). Using Rokeach's Instrumental and Terminal Values Scales, to which the subjects responded by rank-ordering eighteen items, researchers divided the respondents according to such variables as role (student or teacher), age, sex, and teaching or major field. In terms of the composite population (all students versus all faculty) rating the Terminal Values, only five of the eighteen possibilities were assigned the same order by each group. Age group differences were insignificant for the Terminal Values and for the Instrumental Values, although these differences became more apparent when the staff and student values were combined. Again, with sex, similarities between groups were generally greater than differences. "Accordingly, we might hypothesize that the *role* assumed by the faculty or staff member is actually greater than any differences that might appear in terms of his or her sex—that is, when an individual decides to adopt the teaching role (or the role of the educator), he generally becomes more like other teachers, regardless of sex" (pp. 38–39).

In reporting problems in their professional roles, instructors at the three colleges sometimes showed significant differences. For example, the Rural College faculty rated "Lack of time for scholarly study" and "Understanding college policies to be followed in curriculum development and revision" more important than did the faculties of the other two schools. Most faculty members in all three schools feel they should have the major responsibility for educational policy, but they also feel administrative staff must mandate personnel policy. This appears consistent with findings reported from faculties at various other schools.

Faculties' perceptions of why students attend their college showed a wide spread among the schools, even though similar rankings were obtained for "Get training for a job," and differences were no greater than one point for "Parents want them to," "To apply for a student draft deferment," "Get a basic general education and appreciation of ideas," and "Be with friends." Agreement is indicated in only five of fifteen items, suggesting a great disparity in the way faculty judge students' feelings and attitudes.

Faculties in the three colleges showed extreme concern for helping their students achieve goals, but they disagreed about what a community college should help students acquire (Knowledge and skills directly applicable to their careers; An understanding and mastery of some specialized body of knowledge, Preparation for further formal education; Self-knowledge and personal identity, A broad general education, Knowledge of and interest in community and world problems). Faculty respondents were genuinely concerned with their students' learning and their own effects on students, wishing that they had more data on these long-term effects, that students were more inclined to study, and that they had some assurances their students were learning.

In terms of instructional patterns preferred by instructors, faculties in the three colleges differed, particularly regarding preferences for structured or unstructured class discussions, audio-tutorial sessions, and pass-no-credit and ABC-no-credit grading practices. They were more similar in expressing how they see themselves in comparison with the "average junior college teacher" (Commitment to students, Understanding and accepting the junior college philosophy, Knowledge of both subject matter and institutional practices, and Tendencies to alter instruction where appropriate").

This, then, is the way the faculties of three California community colleges measure up along certain selected characteristics. There are some differences among our three subgroups, but, in general, each school seems to have instructors much like those in the other two. Although there is intrainstitutional heterogeneity, interinstitutional differences seem minimal.

Since we conclude that the faculties in all three community colleges are similar, we can consider the conditions and concerns of members of one college faculty as representative of those of community college staff in general. A further study of Suburban College examines the opportunities for faculty innovation and faculty responses to such opportunities.

The study used the participant observation method, which allows the investigator to perceive process, sequence, and change over a period of time (Purdy, 1973). The investigator spent eight months on the college campus, observing instructors in their everyday work, attending formal meetings, participating in informal groups, and interviewing college staff members. She found that there are distinct, consistent teacher types and that campus climate is a tangible force leading to acceptance or rejection of certain innovations by the staff as a whole.

Several administrative practices are designed to promote innovative teaching at Suburban College. A Faculty Fellowship program provides funds for supplies, equipment, and expert assistance. The grants supply the resources and time to encourage an instructor to follow through with a project that a normal teaching load would not allow. Up to twenty fellowships have been granted each year since the program began in 1969, and the support offered by these grants has contributed to the development of courses and programs now seen as models of innovation, such as audio-tutorial biology, the typing laboratory, and computer-assisted instructional course segments in chemistry. In addition, funds are available for summer instructional improvement projects, faculty travel and attendance at conferences, the purchase of instructional hardware, and technical support staff and supply centers to train and assist teachers who are working with technological innovations.

Suburban enjoys its desired reputation for innovation, but innovation of a particular kind. The college was called "Electronic U" by one journalist who suggested that all its teachers utilize technological devices. Visitors see the telecommunications center with its television studio, audio-tutorial labs, computer services center, and library media center. Although decisions to move into all these areas were made at different times and often for unrelated reasons, the total effect is that instruction at Suburban indeed seems an electronic process. And yet, a majority of the instructors teach at least one traditional class using the lecture-discussion method, and perhaps as many as half of the faculty have done little more than dabble in the media. The Suburban College reputation results in part from the fact that technological teaching devices are visible and can be easily demonstrated while nontechnological instructional experiments, such as team teaching and interdisciplinary courses, are less obvious.

Faculty members at Suburban believe they should have jurisdiction over certain areas of their work. They want primary control of their classes—the room, how the course is taught, the textbooks—and partial control over, or at least participation in discussions about, divisional and college matters that affect their work (budget, purchase of new equipment, appointment of a division chairman). Since the instructors are aware that conditions outside their control, such as trustees' decisions, state legislation, and student interests and fads, impinge on their teaching, they understand that they do not have sole authority. But over those areas where they feel they should have primary influence, they are vehement about protecting their work space from interference by anyone.

The phrase *work space* is helpful in representing the faculty domain of influence and authority on the job, but not all faculty members define their work space in the same manner. For example, music teachers feel they should have a say in setting concert dates, prices charged, and policy on music tours, while other instructors are most sensitive about controlling course planning and choosing course materials. Work space also refers to physical location. At Suburban, the math-science and health science teachers have clashed several times over sharing classrooms. Here is a case of faculty impinging on the work space of other faculty; the administration is not the only threat to one's perceived domain.

An instructor's concern with work space is concentric, moving from his own area of control and authority to that of his peers in a subject-matter area, to concern for his division, and finally concern for the collective work space of all instructors on his campus. A basic requirement for faculty job satisfaction is a set of guarantees that protect both collective and individual work space. This protection comes in the form of job contracts and legal guarantees, as well as in informal agreements and arrangements. One hindrance to the formation of a strong faculty organization is that faculty are not willing to give up control over their work space unless they perceive a greater threat to their freedom. A potent faculty organization might be an intrusion. The sensitivity of faculty to infringement on the work space suggests a relationship between faculty autonomy and their acceptance of administration-sponsored innovations. To the extent that administration shows a regard for those areas of an instructor's domain that he feels are crucial, he is likely to accept the administrator's suggestions and hardware.

Since both perceived administrative support and protection of faculty autonomy and faculty attitudes toward innovation run from positive to negative, instructors can be divided into four groups: *uninhibited innovators, hesitant innovators, uninvolved noninnovators, and alienated noninnovators.*

Uninhibited innovators see the administration as supportive, feel their work space is protected, and are enthusiastic about campus innovations. They have developed audio-tutorial courses, labs, computer-assisted instructional programs, and video segments for classes. None have experienced rejection of an idea or proposal, and they have readily taken advantage of the Faculty Fellowships. Quick to credit the administration for the Suburban College reputation as an innovative campus, they have high regard for the administration and freely praise the president and deans for being supportive. Instructors in this group are content because they receive funding, equipment, and administrative encouragement for their projects. But many of them are isolated from their faculty colleagues.

During the early years when they were leaders in changing traditional teaching methods they bore the brunt of much faculty hostility; they needed and received administrative sup-

port. While overt opposition to "impersonal teaching" methods
has largely subsided, and clusters of faculty using audio-tutorial
systems and computers on campus now exist, these faculty members who completely supported the administration tend to be
loners. Some are so because they have been promoted to administrative posts—the Director of Learning Resources or division
chairmanships. Others are loners because they continue to experiment with each new hardware development, thus continuing the work that originally separated them from the majority.
A few seem to be loners by personal choice; they prefer solo
experimenting to team efforts. Their dependence on administrative rather than faculty support can only increase; they realize they need the administration in order to continue their
work.

Hesitant innovators, the majority at Suburban College,
are suspicious of the administration and feel continual vigilance
of faculty autonomy is necessary. They are neutral or in favor
of campus innovations and have tried some of them. Because
they are strongly committed to whatever innovation they work
on they draw a lot of attention to themselves. All are willing to
talk about their newest instructional concerns. Several hold
formal or informal leadership roles with the faculty. All but
one have been at Suburban at least three years and are content,
though not uncritical of the college. Several are active in the
Faculty Senate, and one is a division chairman.

Unlike the uninhibited innovators, the innovators in this
group see fundamental differences in opinion and concerns between the faculty and the college administration. While several
of these instructors are personal friends with individual administrators, they always distinguish administrative from faculty
perspectives. Some distrust all administrators in any school;
others have become suspicious of the motives of specific Suburban administrators. Some perceive a reduction in administrative
support for an innovation they have worked on and therefore
are suspicious of administrative motives in supporting any
innovation.

Some hesitant innovators characterize the administration
as being concerned with appearance, either of being innovative

or of saving money, while the faculty are concerned with whether the innovation is a better instructional method. Some hesitant innovators also believe the administration has been manipulative and devious in working with some teachers. They are cynical regarding administrators' motives and actions, no matter how amiable the relations between the groups. Nevertheless, some members of the group are active and involved teachers whom administrators see as models of creativity.

The hesitant innovators are distinguished from the alienated noninnovators by a feeling of relative security. Accepting that the administration may not be completely trustworthy and should be kept at a distance from the faculty work space, nonetheless, these teachers find a secure enough environment in which to teach as they want. They imply that protection of their work space comes from several sources: large and powerful divisions, division chairmen who defend faculty rights, the potential use of the Senate, personal arrangements such as friendship with one administrator, and establishment of work spaces in which the administration has little interest.

Finally, hesitant innovators highly value colleagueship among teachers. There are no loners in this group as there are among the uninhibited innovators. Where they have experimented with innovations, they have done it in teams. Several are spokesmen for greater faculty participation in governance and are leaders in the Faculty Senate. Several of them may have been uninhibited innovators at one time but, sensing administrative reduction in support of certain innovations in favor of others, have become members of groups pressing for continued administration funds for their work.

Uninvolved noninnovators see the administration as supportive and do not fear interference, but they are uninterested in campus innovations. The group is comprised of two types of faculty: new instructors who have not yet committed themselves to an instructional approach, and older members who use one instructional method only. Many of the new instructors are in awe of all the support services provided faculty and conclude that the administration will do anything to encourage innovation. Some are suspicious of the technology, others are neutral and curious. Most are busy adjusting to their jobs, sometimes their first college position, and have little time left to learn how to use a slide-tape carrousel or write a test to be computerized. The new uninvolved noninnovators do not remain in this category for long but come under the influence of a strong faculty personality who encourages them in one direction or another.

The older faculty in the uninvolved noninnovator group have been teachers for years and at Suburban long enough to establish their reputation for not being interested in any instructional method other than lecture-discussion, book reading, and tests. Some of them are isolated from their peers and apathetic about the whole college atmosphere, though they do not express particular criticism of the innovations, just a lack of interest. And some are respected by their colleagues because they have withstood both peer group and administrative pressure to try some innovative practice. Other faculty consider these traditionalists good at what they do.

Alienated noninnovators feel that administration dominates faculty work space completely, leaving faculty members little autonomy. They are negative toward campus innovations. Few faculty at Suburban can be classified as completely alienated noninnovators. People in this category are uncomfortable and do not stay in it. Some make arrangements to allow themselves acceptable autonomy; others become apathetic. Some quit or are fired. Several faculty members have left the campus apparently because of dislike for the technological emphasis or incompatibility with the administration. Many alienated faculty, those who distrust the administration most, are actually innovators unobtrusively pursuing an instructional approach they consider significantly innovative.

The alienated noninnovators hold strong views on the need of faculty for autonomy in their work. When pressed, one faculty member said that a requirement for job satisfaction is being able to do whatever he wants in the classroom. He is cynical about the effect of new technological media, concluding that they do not make any difference in the area where it matters most—motivating students to learn.

Faculty who have the strongest opinions against the administration and against instructional hardware are well known on campus. Because of their respected academic training, maturity, and ability to articulate their opinions, they are tolerated —perhaps even respected—by the administration and by other instructors. One teacher expressed this basic complaint: "We know what we think is good teaching, but we aren't in a position to make the decisions about where to put the college money because of the governance structure here. So, in effect, the administration makes the decisions of what kind of teaching will be encouraged." If faculty representation in governance becomes a widespread concern on campus, these alienated noninnovators may gain more influence with campus faculty members.

Intrusion on an instructor's work space can come from peers as well as from administrators, therefore the faculty culture contains provisions that set limits on colleagues. In divisions and subgroups teachers maintain the rules, alliances, and compromises that protect them from each other. The actual functioning of the means of protection can best be seen in the day-to-day discussions and negotiations between individuals and groups over working conditions, rules of work, and control of equipment and space.

The most commonly known informal restriction on teachers is the prohibition against observing another teacher in the classroom unless given an invitation or specific advance approval by the teacher to be observed. An instructor's immediate peer group and even the larger faculty reference group at the college have other methods as well. The peer group can provide instructors information or deprive them of it by filtering or distorting that information. Teachers hearing about instructional innovations through colleagues give the ideas more serious consideration than if the information comes from nonteachers. The campus grapevine is seen as more reliable than any other source.

Faculty peer groups have more influence than just that over the contents and accuracy of information, however. The groups have powerful sanctions that influence an individual's behavior and ideas. Such influence can inhibit or suppress a teacher who wants to experiment or deviate from group norms, but it can also create support for teachers when a change in practices is considered. If an instructor who wants to experiment can find a few colleagues interested in the innovation, a group is formed that both supports the members and protects them from other teachers' criticism. Faculty members experimenting with new instructional methods require more moral support than do instructors who are working in familiar and approved ways.

Faculty subgroups may be permanent or fluid; they may be based on a teaching discipline, a teaching style, or a political necessity, as when equipment must be purchased and controlled. They also cooperate with administrators, counseling staff, student groups, or support staff in trying to achieve certain ends.

The discovery of the many functions served by faculty subgroups conflicts with the traditional hierarchical model of educational organizations, which holds that purposive change must be introduced at the top of the organization and filter down, and that changes introduced at lower levels compete or conflict with basic organizational goals.

Based on the research at Suburban College, Baldridge's (1972) model of internal power blocs and interest groups seems a realistic picture of community college organization. For example, although the Suburban administration wields considerable power, part of its success at introducing innovations is due to its alliances with various subgroups on campus. It always knows of instructors who are anxious to use the media and hardware before the materials arrive on campus. These instructors, rather than the administration, become the advocates of the innovations. Here an alliance is formed that is useful to both sides: the teachers get the funds and equipment to experiment with new media while the administration introduces innovations without appearing autocratic.

Thus, Suburban College is an organization consisting of fluid groups, conflicts, alliances, and compromises by which the organization changes. What is important to a teacher's sense of security is that at any one time he believes that his group has the potential or actual power to protect his own work space. Otherwise, that person concentrates energy and resources on opposing threats to his domain. The alienated noninnovators perceive inadequate autonomy in their work space, and thus remain either active in opposition to all administratively backed methods of teaching or apathetic toward them.

Innovations affect faculty work space and relations with administrators and other teachers. The administration provides the funds, equipment, hardware, and technical staff. In return they want to see the results of their expenditures, so they arrange more visitations and observations and more tests and measurements of student learning. Administrators also set up rules for use of the new equipment, rules that draw teachers and their students out of separate classrooms and labs into media centers.

In addition to greater exposure to and interference from administrators, the innovations also require greater exposure to other teachers, which for some instructors is as threatening as administrative inspection. Many new methods require team teaching or group commitment. For example, introductory courses in an audio-tutorial arrangement may have a large group lecture and small discussion groups, or open labs, where two or three teachers and aides rotate in handling students' questions, displays, assignments, and problems with equipment. Thus, only one teacher assumes the traditional role of lecturer and the rest cooperate to plan the course. Gone is the solo practitioner who taught introductory composition as he desired regardless of how ten other introductory courses were taught.

In summary, changing instructional practices is clearly not as simple as purchasing new equipment or sending a teacher to a workshop on the merits of a new technique. Before instructors adopt instructional practices foreign to them, they need a sense of autonomy in their work situation and the support and protection of their peers. We do not mean that there is an absolute and ideal level of autonomy for all teachers or that the more autonomy teachers have, the more they will experiment. To be willing to experiment, teachers first have to be satisfactorily assured that they have the option of choosing whatever technique they believe to be best—in other words, to be certain their work space is not violated. The institutional supports, while necessary, are of secondary importance.

Many administrators believe that a teaching innovation has been introduced successfully if they set up some hardware and see a few students using it (learning-resource centers are frequently examples). But unless the faculty perceive the innovation as a useful device and incorporate it in their teaching, it remains an adjunct, doomed to remain on the periphery.

Administrators who succeed in encouraging sizable numbers of instructors to adopt new techniques respect the faculty work space. They set a climate that allows instructors to take the lead, allowing time for the adoption process to run its course. They do not badger the nonacceptors but try rather to understand what the proposed innovation means to these people. In short, they respect the instructors as colleagues.

The choice of instructional methods, probably the most basic part of an instructor's work, is not the private personal decision many teachers would like to think it is. The more the method being considered requires institutionally provided equipment, staff assistance, peer cooperation, and time and space in which to experiment, the more the decision becomes a shared one involving many groups in the institution. Because the boundary between administrative and faculty responsibility for the instructional process is not easily determined, teachers, through negotiations, must formulate the conditions under which they will experiment with and adopt new practices.

Chapter Ten

Increasing Job Satisfaction

The problem of job satisfaction touches everyone and is important not only for the employee but also for the employer, because workers who like their jobs will work with efficiency and enthusiasm—the dissatisfied ones will not.

Personal satisfaction with one's work is a familiar topic in industrial psychology. For decades researchers have tried to understand employee morale and to establish relationships between job satisfaction and productivity, absenteeism, and other effects. But a parallel line has not been pursued in the study of higher education. Professors do not characterize themselves as "workers"; hence, they infrequently look to the literature of business and industry for models or theories for describing their activities. And indices of productivity—the result typically judged in industry—are weak in higher education. The number of research studies and scholarly publications produced by professors can be counted along with the number of hours per week they spend in teaching, but the quality of the product in both cases is difficult to ascertain and nearly impossible to attribute to any characteristic of the organizational environment.

Still, there are criteria, perhaps imprecise, that will indicate the degree to which educators find job satisfaction. One could say that a college with an enthusiastic, personally satisfied staff is more likely to further student development than is one with an apathetic group of time-servers going through the motions of information transmittal in their teaching. But students are not the only people on campus. The recent high level of interest in worker satisfaction in other industries suggests that a shift in social outlook is occurring, with employees becoming more concerned with their immediate working environment and expecting more from their jobs than mere subsistence (*Work in America,* 1973). As they realize the importance of the job to their own sense of well-being and personal identity, they become unwilling to submit to less than convivial conditions in the work place. Gibson and Teasley (1973) suggest that a primary function of an organization should be the "satisfaction of member needs." Along with workers in other contexts— and not withstanding the institutional-level rhetoric about selfless dedication to students—college faculty members are becoming increasingly attentive to their work milieu.

The acceleration in number of college faculty members working under contracts derived through collective bargaining processes points to this growing concern for the work environment. Invariably these contracts include more than statements of wages and fringe benefits; throughout, they address working conditions, particularly supervisory and grievance procedures, and provide specification as to the types of institutional assistance to be afforded the professors. There is more to these agreements than a mere shift in locus of control from administrators to faculty members; they reveal a concern for teacher welfare in the broadest use of the term.

Collective bargaining has made its greatest inroads in higher education among community college faculty members. If the experience of negotiated contracts in other industries is any guide to the pattern, concern for worker satisfaction as evidenced by bargaining for changed working conditions will come rapidly to the fore in these colleges. Representative groups will move quickly past negotiating for wages and fringe benefits to specifying patterns of supervision, space allocation, and other characteristics of the work environment.

But how will the impending changes in institutional milieu affect the community college instructors? Little is known now about the motivational aspects of their job and the studies that have been done cluster around variant sets of assumptions.

The work environment was defined by Lofquist and Dawis (1969) as the setting in which work behavior takes place. This setting may be described in several ways. The traditional approach takes the point of view of the employer, using such categories as tasks to be performed, working conditions, tools and materials used, and economic benefits. In this scheme, the basic concept is the job or position, which is a set of tasks done by the worker. The sociological approach incorporates the idea of position but enlarges it to include not only tasks, but dimensions such as power, prestige, and goals. It also looks at the environment in terms of subcultures and formal-informal organization. The psychological approach studies the environment through workers' behavior and point of view. This is done through an analysis of the worker's personality traits, attitudes and values, and perceptions of the environment, or, quite frequently, by focusing on the sources of his satisfactions and dissatisfactions.

Each point of view—the traditional, sociological, and psychological—has been used at one time or another to categorize community colleges as a work environment. The traditional model, for example, is found in community college collective bargaining agreements, which define the tasks of the faculty, their working conditions, and economic benefits they will accrue. Although content varies from contract to contract, most carefully describe the tasks of instructors to include meetings with students inside and outside of class, participation in course and curriculum development, attendance at faculty-administration meetings, and selection of department chairmen, whose tasks are also outlined.

The working conditions of faculty are delineated in terms of class assignments and size, the definition of the work week and the college calendar, the size and availability of faculty offices, the provision for released time for meetings and administrative duties, the use of college facilities, and the procedures for grievances. In addition, provisions for instructional support services are usually included, such as secretarial and paraprofessional help and media centers.

Economic factors found in the bargaining agreements include conditions of employment such as contracts, probation, evaluation, promotion, demotion, seniority, tenure, and retirement. Salary schedules, some with provisions for overtime pay, are almost always included. Conditions for outside employment, travel reimbursements, sabbatical and other leaves, holidays, and insurance are spelled out.

The sociological approach to the junior college environment is illustrated by two studies, both of which analyze the dimension of power attached to the faculty position. Barrett (1969), in his investigation of North Carolina community colleges, found that power and job satisfaction seem to be related. When the faculty perceived an increase in their ability to make decisions concerning their college, their degree of job satisfaction was increased. Blackburn and Bylsma (1970) studied power as it is affected by collective bargaining. Their analysis of six Michigan junior colleges suggests that, since the onset of collective bargaining in 1965, the decision-making power of the faculty increased in all areas relating to their welfare, such as class size, workload, and salaries. However, while it diffused the decision-making process by involving faculty in decisions, collective bargaining also resulted in a more tightly structured bureaucracy, because it specifically defined faculty and administrator roles. The size of the institution and the affiliation of the bargaining unit were unrelated to the changes that occurred.

The psychological approach has been taken by several analysts of the community college environment. Garrison (1967) concluded that the attitudes of most junior college instructors are student-centered and pragmatic; they evaluate their teaching according to the competency of their graduates and feel that the junior college should help students acquire skills useful to their careers. Koile and Tatem (1966), in a comparison of junior college and four-year college faculty, substantiated

Garrison's conclusion. Eighty-four percent of their subjects ranked teaching as their first preferred activity, as compared to far fewer at the four-year level. Further support of the importance of the student-centered values of junior college instructors was given in Blai's study (1972) at Harcum Junior College in Pennsylvania. The Harcum faculty rated the problems surrounding the effective teaching of students as their first concern.

Theoretical questions aside, to what extent do two-year college faculty members feel satisfied with their job now? More than 85 percent of the Minnesota instructors surveyed by Eckert and Williams (1972) and 95 percent of the Florida faculty studied by Kurth and Mills (1968) voiced satisfaction. These figures are somewhat higher than those obtained in two studies done during the late 1950s by Medsker (1960) and Eckert and Stecklein (1959). Although comparisons must be made with caution because the data were compiled differently, some increase in satisfaction in the past decade seems evident. For one thing, considerably fewer instructors feel they would rather be in a four-year college or university.

We have some indirect measures of junior college faculty satisfaction as well. A study conducted by the AAJC in 1971 (Bushnell, 1973) asked a national sample of faculty members to rank the goals of the community college in accordance with the way those goals were treated "at the present time" and also to rank them in accordance with the faculty's "preference." The difference between the "present" and "preferred" listings is instructive. Several of the goals showed wide variation between the lists, indicating that faculty would prefer their institutions adopted different policies. This suggests some measure of dissatisfaction with institutional goals.

The generalized satisfaction revealed in the Minnesota and Florida studies or generalized dissatisfaction as manifest in the AAJC national sample presents one picture of faculty satisfaction. However, this satisfaction is not necessarily amenable to change. Rather, it may pertain to the instructor's age, teaching field, and locale. Poosawtsee found the older teachers in Minnesota more satisfied than the young, vocational instructors more satisfied than their academic colleagues, instructors in rural areas

more so than those in the cities ("Which Faculty Members. . . ,"
1974). Barber (1971) discovered that tenured faculty placed more
importance on security benefits and less on salary supplements
than did their nontenured counterparts and that faculty recruited from secondary schools placed less emphasis on research
benefits than did those from business, college teaching, or recent
college graduation. Kurth and Mills (1968) compared satisfied
and dissatisfied teachers and found that the former tend to be
female, older, married, and from rural backgrounds. Obviously,
if these are the controlling variables, nothing can be done
directly to enhance the satisfaction felt by instructors.

A more fruitful line of study seems to involve the instructor's immediate environment. What pleases him in his own
work? What are the intrinsic rewards? What brings discomfort
or frustration? Above all, what in his environment is amenable
to change?

In the literature of industry the traditional approach to
studying job satisfaction is to identify the characteristics of the
job that are satisfying to the worker and to hypothesize that if
these characteristics are enhanced, the worker will become more
satisfied, while if they are reduced, he will tend toward dissatisfaction (Carroll, 1969). Thus, if money is seen as contributing
to satisfaction, more money should lead to greater satisfaction
and less money to dissatisfaction. But this approach has been
challenged because it fails to take expectations into account.
For example, if an employee anticipates a 6 percent increase in
salary but receives only a 2 percent increase, he may be dissatisfied even though he has received more pay. The traditional
approach has also been criticized as too simplistic, that is, perhaps satisfaction and dissatisfaction are not polar opposites and
the same factors do not propel the worker in one direction or
the other.

The idea of satisfaction and dissatisfaction as two different dimensions is postulated by Herzberg and others (1959) who
claim that those elements leading to satisfaction are related to
the actual content of the work, whereas the qualities of the job
leading to dissatisfaction are associated with the environment
surrounding the worker. Thus, those things that the worker

himself does tend toward satisfaction, while dissatisfaction is ascribed to company policy, administration, supervision, and working conditions. The "two-factor" theory, then, separates satisfaction and dissatisfaction by relating the first to "intrinsic factors" or "motivators" and the second to "extrinsic factors" or "hygienes."

The two-factor theory stimulated a number of studies, many of which used the critical incident technique that Herzberg had employed in his own studies. Some studies supported Herzberg's conclusions but others failed to repeat his findings. His thesis has been challenged by some researchers; Beer (1966), for example, states that the problem is "too complex to be explained by global theories and oversimplified models." Gibson and Teasley (1973) review several studies and conclude that "the range of findings run from general support for the two-factor theory, . . . through the finding that subjects were equally satisfied with motivator and hygiene aspects of their jobs, . . . to a vigorous condemnation of Herzberg's methodology, . . . and finally to the conclusion that the two-factor theory is 'grossly oversimplified' and should 'be laid to rest' " (p. 92).

Nevertheless, although the traditional approach and the two-factor theory both have their detractors, it does seem useful to test them in the community college as a means of learning more about faculty members and the college as a work environment. If the traditional approach to studying worker satisfaction holds, that which dissatisfies the community college faculty member should be the opposite of that which satisfies him, and any characteristic of the job may prove to be pertinent. If the two-factor theory holds, then satisfaction should be related to intrinsics while dissatisfaction should be associated with extrinsics.

Data collected in several studies (Cohen, 1973b) used populations comprised of fifty-seven instructors from a small college in southern California, nineteen instructors from nine colleges in Virginia and Maryland, one hundred forty-six instructors from a larger college in northern California, and eighty-two instructors from five colleges in Oregon and Washington.

Three of these groups of instructors were asked to relate one incident that made them pleased with their work, one thing that happened in the previous year that made them satisfied or comfortable with their jobs. As soon as they had completed that task they were asked to write down one incident that tended to displease them, one thing that happened related to their work which had made them dissatisfied or discontent. (The largest group was randomly divided into two subgroups with one asked to respond to the question on satisfaction, the other to respond to the question on dissatisfaction).

Most of the instructors found satisfaction in feedback from their students. When the responses having to do with student learning are combined with those indicating student approval of the instructor, more than 70 percent of the faculty in the Oregon-Washington group and in the two California colleges and more than 50 percent of the Virginia-Maryland group revealed gaining satisfaction from something to do with students. But only about 30 percent of the instructors suggested that dissatisfaction was related to their students. Instead, extrinsic variables, such as lack of support or interference from administrators or colleagues and institutional red tape, were noted as prime annoyances.

In another study, Wozniak (1973) investigated satisfaction among the music faculty in sixty-four two-year colleges. She also found the determinants of job satisfaction to be qualitatively different from the sources of dissatisfaction, reporting that the strongest motivators were achievement, recognition, responsibility, the work itself, and relations with students. Dissatisfaction resulted from working conditions, supervision, and policy and administration, among others.

These results are not surprising. Work satisfaction for a professional group often comes from ministering to clients, a process Sanford (1971) calls "the most elementary satisfaction of professional activity." Community college instructors are professional teachers and see interaction with students as their main purpose. Garrison (1967) found "genuine enthusiasm for teaching undergraduates and for working with them individually." Park (1971) reported this same commitment to students among faculty in three California community colleges. Interaction with students comes forward as the chief intrinsic motivator.

What can be done to enhance satisfaction? Brown and Shukraft (1971) note that "self-reflection, while a necessary step, is rarely sufficient to bring about change in the life of the person unless the social environment is supportive of such change. Just as there are mutually reinforcing aspects in the role of professor and student, there are reinforcing and constraining influences in the culture of a particular faculty" (p. 203). And Guion (1974) says, "Job satisfaction is a highly personal, subjective construct; different people react to the same organizational stimuli with different kinds and degrees of affect. Organizational climate, however, should be consistently perceived by different people; it is more objective. Climate is an organizational characteristic; satisfaction is an individual characteristic" (p. 294). In other words, if the variables leading to satisfaction in one's work are intrinsic and—in the case of community college instructors—related to faculty-student interaction, then satisfaction can be best enhanced by removing obstacles to this interaction. This can be accomplished most readily by mandating smaller classes, allocating aides to assist instructors with routine management chores, and providing economic security so that instructors are freed from concern about lower-order needs—what instructors, through their professional associations, have been clamoring for for years.

Staff satisfaction cannot be ignored. The rapidly expanding unions are demanding that the institutions be, in effect, more satisfying places in which to work. And Jencks and others (1972) argue that instead of evaluating schools on the basis of their long-term effects, we might better evaluate them "in terms of their immediate effects on teachers and students. . . . Some schools are dull, depressing, even terrifying places, while others are lively, comfortable, and reassuring. If we think of school life as an end in itself rather than a means to some other end, such differences are enormously important" (p. 7). Further, the colleges are in an era of low growth. Few new staff are being employed, and, with jobs hard to find, few are leaving. It has become nearly impossible to dismiss the disgruntled instructor, to encourage him to resign, or to shunt him to a quiet corner while handing over his responsibilities to a new staff member. Whether or not community college leaders feel their institutions should strive to enhance faculty satisfaction, the issue is before them.

Some forward-looking administrators have addressed the issue. The Macomb County Community College board adopted a resolution that stated in part: the college "is in the business of enabling persons to become all they are capable of becoming. We cannot promise these enabling mechanisms to our students without also providing them to our employees. . . . Employee satisfaction with the work situation is one of our equal opportunity goals." However, in many other institutions, satisfaction seems subsidiary to staff development, retraining, reassignment, and a host of other variables.

But what of that elusive factor, student learning? The assumption that satisfaction leads to better job performance is based on the belief that the satisfied worker is intrinsically motivated to produce. But do community college instructors feel that what they are to produce is student learning? To an instructor, teaching may mean anything from arranging a sequence of events deliberately so that learning occurs to interacting with students and hoping something useful results. On one end of the continuum is a process specifically designed to attain its purpose; on the other is an activity that may or may not lead to definable effect (with no presumption that learning will result).

These variant definitions of teaching are revealed in the data from the Cohen studies. Statements about student learning ("class grade average higher than anticipated," "students created a high quality product") and reports of student expressions of approval of the instructor ("student told me he liked the course," "student brought me roses") each received an approximately equal number of responses (thirty-nine versus thirty-one). Both results seem to satisfy, with the instructor's choice probably depending on the definition of teaching to which he or she subscribes.

The large number of responses in which students expressed approval of the instructor with no reported evidence of learning tends to support the findings of a prior study of three California community colleges in which most instructors thought the students looked first for "instructors' personality" when they entered a class and felt students would like them to "be available for individual conferences" (Cohen, 1970). There is some question as to whether this pattern of self-centeredness is related to instructors' desires to see students learn or whether it is a separate dimension.

One might hope that "interaction with students" as an intrinsic motivator would be supplanted in the mind of the instructor by "student learning." Faculty would then support better testing procedures and student follow-up studies in order to gain more precise data on effects. But many faculty seem to think that if students learn, they—the instructors—contributed to the learning, while faculty members rarely blame themselves if students fail to learn (students are then seen as unprepared, uninterested, or unmotivated). Faculty have not attained the truly professional status exemplified by understanding and accepting responsibility for effects on clients—positive and negative.

Faculty evaluation, in-service training, and similar administrative attempts to influence instructor behavior have little effect unless combined with institutional support for faculty endeavors. Any extrinsic index of productivity is meaningless. Counting the hours instructors spend on the job or evaluating them by observing them in the classroom may satisfy external auditors, but it does not directly affect instructor motivation. It is most important to understand what faculty themselves feel they are producing. Only this factor can be appropriately linked to the instructors' satisfaction with their work because it is the only one they truly consider.

Chapter Eleven

Relating Tenure, Evaluation, Faculty Development

Evaluating faculty members is as old as the schools, all of which have formal procedures for rating the staff. Even so, everyone sees it differently. To administrators the process has been useful for communicating policies and for maintaining their own files about what is going on in the classroom. To instructors it may be a nuisance, an interruption of no consequence, or an opportunity to show what they have done. Periodically, outsiders—trustees, legislators, the lay public—become incensed over some indiscretion that one instructor or a group of them has committed and demand more stringent procedures to weed out the unfit, the malcontents, the deviants. They call this evaluation, too.

A bill requiring regular evaluation of all staff—tenured and nontenured alike—was passed in California in 1971. Reactions were varied and intense. Some administrators thought that evaluation had attained a new dimension, that they had been given the right to dismiss bad teachers. Indeed, the push for the bill came from people who intended just that. Instructors felt they had lost a large measure of security because the bill seemed to strike at the heart of tenure itself with its mechanisms for employee review, rating, and dismissal. But the intervening years have proved both groups wrong. That California community colleges roll along much as before is not surprising to the observer of institutions who knows that no one law can change their basic structure.

The concept of tenure rests on several premises: university professors need it to protect their pursuit of truth through research; community college instructors who espouse unconventional beliefs must be shielded from those who cannot tolerate heretics; deviant behavior inside or outside the classroom at any level of schooling should not be cause for dismissal. Triggered in part by student activism, attacks on tenure came in waves in the early 1970s. The student protests against numerous social ills had been greeted negatively by a majority of laymen who saw professors as culpable. Even if professors did not openly support the activism, the reasoning went, they condoned it. As a result, a variety of antagonists to tenure clustered around the argument that those who affront prevailing mores should not be shielded indiscriminately. And although activism was rampant in only a few two-year colleges, the characterization of these institutions as part of higher education made them party to the charge.

A second input to lay rejection of the tenure principle is that people who are involved with an institution typically feel they should have a say in how that institution is managed, what its purposes should be, what qualifications should mark its personnel. When colleges enrolled a small percentage of the population, they were responsive primarily to the members of that group—their alumni and the social strata they represented. As the colleges broadened the social base from which they drew their clients, they invited new groups to question the institution itself. And one of the first questions raised was, "Why should faculty have jobs guaranteed for life when I enjoy nothing of the sort?"

Yet another reason tenure fell into disfavor was—and is —the supply of qualified staff as related to job openings. In the early 1960s, when a teacher shortage was prevalent, the problem was seen as one of need. Anyone with a credential was employed. A decade later, well-qualified young people were available in large numbers. The concern of governing boards and administrators then became how to make room for them, what to do about the older instructors whose courses were no longer popular and who refused to innovate in their teaching methods —the "deadwood."

These areas of disaffection with tenure led to various forms of action, as in Virginia where in 1973 a system of fixed-time contracts was adopted. But the attempts to abolish or circumvent tenure came when workers in other fields were gaining guaranteed annual wages, continuing contracts, and a set of procedures that maintain their employment through due process. This mitigated the pressure on instructors. And those who would place them at the mercy of governing boards, legislators, or lay committees to dismiss at will were stopped for an even more basic reason: the system protects its own. Collegiate ranks cannot be breached on the issue of job security unless the attackers are willing to totally reform the institution itself—its purposes, control, managerial procedures, community and internal relations—and this they are not ready to do.

Nevertheless, the assault on tenure has had some important effects. Early retirement plans have been formulated in many districts, thus allowing both severance by mutual consent without loss of face and a more flexible pattern of retention and dismissal. Faculty unionism has been given a boost as organizers have emphasized the need for collective security. The lingering vestiges of paternalism have been dealt a mortal blow as administrators find the courts ready to restrict their previously discretionary powers. And faculty evaluation, for decades an inconsequential practice, has been given new life.

Historically, evaluation has not been used to determine which instructors should be dismissed. Evidence of conduct that warrants a person's severance from the organization has never originated with the evaluation process. Instead, it arises from the chance remark in the coffee shop, the phone call from the irate parent, the student complaint, the vendetta pursued by a jealous or vengeful colleague, the manifestation of sullenness or derisive behavior in committee meetings. In all cases where information acquired through formal evaluations *has* been introduced in dismissal proceedings it has, in fact, represented little more than a bureaucratic smokescreen behind which the inquisitors have hidden.

If faculty evaluation has not been used to dismiss alleged ne'er-do-wells, what has it done? Primarily it has advanced the illusion of professionalism. That is, it has made it appear as though educators were policing their own ranks, insuring that each member pulled his share of the load, weeding out the unworthy. But educators have not done this previously, they are not doing it now, and, legislative fiat to the contrary notwithstanding, they will not do it in the near future.

Faculty evaluation has never been crucial to institutional functioning. Where the instructor has not been protected by due process, where he has been subject to dismissal at the will of the trustees and administrators, formal evaluation has been little more than an excuse that allows the managers to do what they want. And where faculty members *have* been protected by some form of tenure, evaluation has been a sterile exercise. As long as the evaluator had no power over the instructor, who cared about it? Small wonder that faculty evaluation remained in the doldrums. It was supposed to lead to improvement of instruction and to greater instructor effort and achievement by virtue of its pointing up models of good instructors and exemplary teaching practices, but few believed in its usefulness. In short, because it was ineffectual it was ignored.

So, in order to find a process for identifying and dismissing unworthy instructors that would stand up in court, the California legislature passed a bill mandating that every junior college district in the state come up with its own evaluation plan within certain guidelines. This triggered a flurry of activity on the campuses—committees were formed, reports were written and circulated, and discussions were initiated. Within a year, all the districts had generated revised plans—some of them as much as 130 pages long.

Little is to be learned by reviewing the many plans that were produced in response to the legislation. Suffice to say that they differ from the procedures in operation a year earlier primarily in that they state specific guidelines for the involvement of the various groups on campus. Indeed this "must" was written into the legislation—students, faculty members, administrators, and the instructor himself should all have a say in each faculty member's evaluation. Other than that difference—which took evaluation out of the sole hands of the administration—little has been added that is new except for extensive committee review and checkback procedures. However, one element has been notably deemphasized—the classroom visitation by the division chairman or dean, which was formerly the primary source of evaluation. This has taken its place as only one of many elements of a thorough evaluation, including, for example, examination of the instructor's course objectives, perusal of student rating forms, and self-evaluation reports submitted by the instructor.

The new plans have had little effect on faculty dismissal. The first line of defense of tenure was breached when all instructors became subject to review, but several others were quickly erected. The courts have ruled that before an instructor can be dismissed the college must produce precise job descriptions detailing his responsibilities (three years after the legislation only half the California colleges had them) and show exactly how he failed to discharge them. And the college must show how it tried to help the instructor overcome his shortcomings (even fewer colleges have systematic procedures for continuous staff training, counseling, or other forms of professional aid). It remains about as difficult as before to remove a staff member who does not want to leave.

If evaluation is of little use in dismissal proceedings, what good is it? It is useful only when it is separated from issues of promotion and severance. Evaluation should enhance the growth of the individual faculty member as a human being. An individual's occupation is a major influence on the sort of person he becomes. Peer values, the demands of group leaders, and the environment in which he works can solidify a person's own belief systems. They can also create conflicts that delay growth and, in fact, warp personal development. Faculty evaluation practices are nothing less than reflections of group values. If the environment in which a person works is not perceived as supportive, then dissatisfaction, stricture, and arrested self-development may well ensue.

Most college personnel policy statements note something to the effect that, "Once an instructor has been employed, the presumption is that he will prove satisfactory; to this end, evaluation should be helpful and supportive." If this means what it says, and if each individual perceives the process as helpful and supportive, it can assist each instructor's own development as a mature, well-functioning human being. If, however, an instructor feels put upon by the way the evaluation procedure is employed, it can warp his growth.

In addition to promoting the instructor's growth, a faculty evaluation plan must (at least indirectly) enhance student learning. Faculty evaluation cannot of itself manipulate the conditions leading to student achievement, but it can be influential in guiding the instructor toward a state of mind in which he wants to create better learning conditions. The instructor who feels that his colleagues are trying to help him teach better may well address himself more vigorously to that part of his work.

Any viable evaluation procedure must also accommodate all campus groups. The students have a stake in the evaluation of their teachers. Student rating forms, student written reports, and student participation in evaluation committees can all be useful.

Finally, faculty evaluation should reveal institutional values. Some statements, for example include the words, "Specific objectives and course goals shall be submitted to the evaluation committee by the instructor." Such a statement indicates that the values of that college include defined outcomes as an important element in instruction. Here is a significant departure from evaluation procedures that are based primarily, if not exclusively, on classroom observations—the practice where one person sits and watches another perform. The fact that now the instructor is to submit his objectives for scrutiny by his colleagues suggests a shift in emphasis from the teacher's performance to the learning outcomes toward which he strives. Knowledge of what the institution deems important can be quite influential. And when the instructor must reveal specific, measurable instructional objectives for his own use, for use by his students, and as a way of communicating his real intent to his colleagues, he may well recognize their importance.

In other words, the evaluation process is an ideally suited form of intracampus communication. It provides a situation in which alternative objectives and instructional strategies can be discussed, where the success obtained through using one or another instructional technique can be examined. Here is where an instructor can learn what his fellows have tried, and by attending to their comments about his own methods he can incorporate these varied procedures. Nevertheless, this result is difficult to obtain because, as Bennis (1972) put it, many people have chosen to teach in college primarily "because they preferred a low influence environment. . . . They have a low need for structure above them; they do not want to structure the lives of people beneath them." This may be a basic reason for instructors' failure to specify precise objectives. Defining the parameters of student learning approximates structuring peoples' lives. And presenting evidence of student achievement to a supervisor or peer sounds suspiciously like accommodation to a structure above.

Many policy statements address another premise quite directly when they say, "Evaluation should be a record of what people do or fail to do, rather than what they are." This is crucial. Evaluation must not judge the person; it must relate to his effects. Granted that the two are so intertwined they cannot be absolutely separated, the emphasis must still be on the teaching, not the teacher. The ultimate goal of all faculty evaluation processes should be the development of the instructor as a professional person. The professional instructor wants to cause learning. He recognizes that his own worth depends on his successful effects. Evaluation practices, then, that scrutinize *him* rather than his products are anathema. He welcomes evaluation of his effects but rightfully shuns procedures that attend to his smile, his posture, or his voice modulation. The phrase "what people do" should mean the effects they have on their client population; it should not refer to their mannerisms.

Ultimately, all faculty evaluation turns on self-evaluation. In fact, without self-evaluation, all else is meaningless. Yet how is this to be fostered? Self-evaluation must rest on knowledge of one's functioning as a professional person. And in a service or helping profession such as teaching, one's functioning must be measured against one's effects on clients. Knowledgeable deans and division chairmen recognize the truth of this premise but rarely take steps necessary to implement its implied message. Self-evaluation is a personal matter, but institutional procedures as implemented by faculty supervisors can assist in bringing meaning to such evaluation. One way of measuring effects is through collecting evidence about student learning and building it into a formal evaluation procedure. Each instructor can be encouraged by the administration to collect information on short-term learning through pre- and postunit tests and on long-term learning by means of follow-up studies. He can then estimate the results obtained through his instructional efforts and so assess himself. As Shawl (1972) has noted, "The awareness of what his students have learned frees the instructor from all other evaluation processes."

In other words, the evaluation procedure can have positive impact on an instructor's perception of self by leading him to examine his own effects. It can provide a structure through which he gains confirmation as to the efficacy of his work and its relationship to the broader aims of the institution. It can suggest results to watch for so that he collects meaningful data, and it can suggest simplified ways of collecting that information. It can communicate institutional values so that he can assess the correspondence between his own targets and those of the college community. And it can prod him should he feel too busy to evaluate himself or if he has fallen into a rut of doing the same thing over the years. In sum, a faculty evaluation scheme can lend direction to the process of self-evaluation.

Evaluation must not be normative. That is, the evaluators should make no attempt to compare one instructor with another. Each instructor is an individual with his own record of successes and failures, his own trials and errors, and should be judged against himself rather than against others. His individual accomplishments should be the sole measure of his professional functioning.

Nor should all people be expected to be expert in all areas. Service to the college and to the community may be one person's chief strength while another's is student guidance or the defining of varied and well-sequenced instructional objectives. Still another person may be an expert in preparing reproducible instructional media. In consultation with his colleagues and with knowledge gained from examining his own effects, each instructor can judge for himself the area in which he can make the greatest contribution.

Nor should an evaluation scheme be seen as a device that will crank and churn and automatically spew out the miscreants. For no matter how many safeguards, feedback loops, and protective devices are built in, if the intent of evaluation is to get rid of deviants, the scheme will fail because, by its very nature, it will foster a climate of suspicion among the majority of instructors. Even if a policy statement does not say that those who drafted it anticipate using it as a device to eliminate undesirable instructors, if it is so perceived, the entire process is doomed.

Faculty evaluation does relate to dismissal procedures but not in the way many people think. The evaluation process provides data showing precisely how the institution attempted to assist the instructor, which then becomes one source of input if dismissal proceedings must be instigated. But faculty leaders and administrators should not allow this rare use of the information acquired to influence the structure of the evaluation process itself.

In sum, there will always be faculty evaluation schemes in all community colleges—first, because there always have been; second, because in many states it's the law. But in most colleges confusion remains as to the intent of the evaluation process. In reading formal guidelines, one senses an attempt by colleges to straddle a position of policing faculty and a position of improving the professional well-being of individual instructors. One faculty evaluation scheme cannot both judge and assist. Gathering evidence for dismissal is different from supporting, communicating, and inducing growth. Institutional leaders who understand the difference between judgment and assistance can develop a two-stage process—the judgment portion taking over only after all attempts to assist the individual have failed.

Unless faculty members perceive the evaluation process as useful and relevant to themselves they will ignore it. Thus, all formal evaluation procedures should be directed toward furthering self-evaluation, the only process that can enhance individual identity and professional maturity. To augment their development individual instructors may initiate the process of self-evaluation through defining instructional effects without waiting for institutional mandate.

There are problems in integrating faculty evaluation with faculty development. Few college planners understand the principles involved, thus few colleges have incorporated them (one exception is described by Parsons, 1974). In addition, the faculty member is obliged only to show up for classes and to file certain reports. He is not obliged to use objectives even though he can be required to write them. He is not obliged to employ various media, analyze his test items, score his examinations according to defined criteria, or employ any of the other best principles of instruction. Most important, there is no way he can be forced to accept personal responsibility for student learning. According to contract, the instructor need only be there.

Some progress has been made in gaining a more mature view of community college purposes. Many California administrators who greeted the revised evaluation guidelines joyfully because they felt faculty dismissal proceedings would be facilitated have changed their outlook and have begun to understand the need for more positive measures. Staff retraining and reassignment procedures have been built as an aid to instructors whose teaching areas have fallen into disfavor with students. The tenure principle has been shaken but something far more valuable may supersede it—an emphasis on faculty development in the holistic sense.

Chapter Twelve

The Open Door:
How Much Is Enough?

Community colleges are now accepted as a permanent and useful adjunct to universities, doing many things that universities do not do well. Thus, the colleges are assured a place in every state plan for postsecondary education. Yet major community college spokesmen continually refuse to consider the philosophical bases and contradictions of these colleges, even as they attempt vigorously to expand their "mission." Here we elaborate these philosophical foundations and the contradictions among them.

Consciously held or not, philosophies of education do exist. Every choice—to offer a particular program, to change an instructional form, even to change the style of listing courses in a schedule—influences all other functions. Nothing stands alone. Every time a student is encouraged to pursue one topic and discouraged from pursuing another, or provided with opportunities to study some phenomena but not offered the means of studying others, some philosophy of education is being served, albeit unwittingly.

What does the community college curriculum emphasize?

Does it stress the interests of the individual or the needs of society? Does it confront contemporary problems in the abstract or directly? Is instruction centered around organized disciplines of knowledge? Is it structured on unified learning theory? Community college educators have promised to meet all community educational needs. But how are these needs to be met? What are the choices confronting the decision makers?

Early in the century, Alex Lange and Leonard Koos envisioned a college with a transfer function that would relieve the university of its lower division offerings, with a vocational education function that would satisfy the societal need for manpower and the individual need for a job, one providing general education so that informed citizens could make intelligent choices about their own life and the life of their community, and with a function of helping the individual to grow in his own right. All these major themes can still be discerned in community colleges today.

But there have been a number of national issues that in their time were considered critical problems. The Americanization of immigrants was a critical issue at the turn of the century but had subsided by the time the two-year colleges came to the fore. Nevertheless, it is still with us in slightly altered form: we have native "immigrants" whom we feel it is our duty to acculturate. Democracy versus totalitarianism was a crucial concern in the 1930s and again in the 1950s. This had its effect on curriculum as did the pressing manpower requirements of World War II. And the sciences and languages arose immediately following the Sputnik launch.

We have experienced recurrent crises in personal health. Periodically the national administration becomes exercised over our being overweight, smoking, or ingesting potentially harmful substances, and health education gets a renewed emphasis. In the 1960s ecology was of great concern along with the cry of students that school programs were "irrelevant." More recently the energy crisis has captured our attention. The community colleges have responded to each of these crises in their own way; they have offered new courses and programs and have revised instructional forms.

Yet, this tendency to react causes problems for people in college. The institutional role changes constantly. Just as the process of screening people for universities becomes sharpened, we discover that the colleges are supposed to be in the career education business. Just as we develop useful occupational programs, we find that community service is being hailed as the activity that will usher in the millenium. And at the same time the colleges continue to claim they serve individuals primarily by helping them find their way.

An inability or unwillingness to explore these contradictions marks the rhetoric of the community college field, whose leaders take the removal of all barriers to postsecondary education as an act of faith. Many particularly pursue this ideal, saying that we must "break the access barriers," "make good on the implied promise of the open door," and "meet the higher education needs of everyone." The barriers they would remove are geographical, racial, academic, financial, motivational, and institutional. And the way to remove them, they say, is to obtain sufficient funding to construct new college buildings; pay certain students' tuition and living expenses; properly train teachers, counselors, and administrators; and develop new vocational, remedial, and guidance services. If state and national governments provide these funds, the argument concludes, the goal of universal access to higher education will be realized.

This is an attractive set of premises because it fits squarely with the national dream of egalitarianism. Nevertheless, for a number of reasons that have nothing to do with funding, it is impossible to remove all barriers to postsecondary education. And to say that the goal is incapable of being realized is not a derogation of the premises underlying it. Rather it is a conclusion that is reached as soon as the focus of attention is shifted from advocacy to analysis.

The basic problem with breaking down the barriers is that it eludes measurable limits. Its proponents have not admitted the crucial difference between the nearly infinite possibilities afforded by open access to higher education and the need for finite tangible criteria by which to measure their success in making that education available to those who want it.

Instead, they make it seem as though the barriers will still be in place until everyone has entered college. Some carry the contention even further, saying that all barriers to everyone *completing* a college program must be removed.

Several examples illustrate the futility of attempting to achieve the unbounded objective. "Breaking down the geographical barriers" can be interpreted as putting a college within commuting distance of every potential student. But is it enough to place a campus in the approximate center of every concentration of people? The problem of transportation remains, so free buses are provided. There are those who cannot leave home because of dependent children, which means supplying day care centers. The physically handicapped are still excluded, so a complete roster of televised courses is offered. At what point on this continuum have the geographic barriers been broken?

How do we remove all financial barriers? Keep tuition charges low. But some people cannot afford any tuition. Then charge none. There still remains the potential student who must support a family. Then pay him a living wage for attending school. How long shall this subsidy continue? At what point have the financial barriers been broken?

We must remove the barriers occasioned by an inability to do adequate school work. Open the doors to all, regardless of previous academic achievement. But the students who have always done poorly will quickly fail again. Then grant "pass" grades only. Some of them are so poorly oriented to school they will not stay through a whole semester. Then allow them to withdraw without penalty up to the final day of the term. At what point have the academic barriers been broken?

How many people must attend college in order to be sure the motivational barriers are down? Every American over eighteen years old who does not possess an academic degree or a trades certificate is included in the pool of potential students that college advocates perceive. Must they all be enrolled in college in order to attain the goal? Universal attendance is the only way to be sure that no motivational barriers remain. However, it smacks of mandatory attendance and accordingly runs counter to several other contemporary trends. Admission to college can be viewed as a graduated scale. On one extreme are restrictions based on wealth, previous academic achievement, social class, or some other measure of fitness. On the other end lies mandatory attendance. Neither extreme is acceptable in the current social climate.

When breaking down the barriers is examined as an open-ended goal, many subordinate inconsistencies appear. This seemingly meritorious ideal is full of contradictions. As soon as one barrier is removed, another is revealed. Eliminate the geographical barriers by putting a college within commuting distance of every potential student, and the barrier of untoward previous academic performance remains. Open the doors to all people regardless of their prior school achievement and the barrier of inadequate financial resources on which the student can draw remains. Find a way to subsidize the student while he is enrolled and there still remains the problem of providing a form of curriculum and instruction consistent with his goals and interests. An unending number of difficulties appear, all of which impinge on each other.

A related problem is that a barrier removed from the path of one individual or group may perforce be placed in front of another. When formal instruction degenerates under the impact of a nontraditional clientele, the student who could learn well in a structured situation is penalized. When curriculum is so amorphous that tangible academic objectives disappear, the student whose thinking would be challenged by the study of great works suffers. When college resources are used to recruit students from one social or economic group, members of other groups may feel unwelcome or believe that the college is not likely to enhance their own growth.

Mindless of the inconsistencies in their position, many community college spokesmen act as though all should attend who can in any measure profit from even the most minimal exposure to college: "The concept of accountability demands active efforts to seek, recruit, enroll, and retain every possible student in the community" say Roueche, Baker, and Brownell (1971, p. 11). Their demand is being met enthusiastically with intensive student recruiting and attempts to introduce an unending series of new experiences within the colleges regardless of their intrinsic merit.

People have certain needs—physical, psychological, social—that must be satisfied. But only when a need is perceived does it become a want. Do people *need* to go to college or do they *want* to go? Assuming they want to, to what extent is this desire stimulated by forces external to the schools and how much of it can be attributed to demand stimulation by the colleges? Suffice to say here that vigorous recruiting campaigns and massive marketing operations are an integral part of college activities.

From the institutional standpoint, students must be enticed to the campus if the decline in the birthrate that began in the late 1950s is to present no problem to future institutional growth. So-called new students must fill vacant places if enrollments are to continue increasing. These potential students, made up of minority group members who heretofore have not enrolled, adults who missed the chance to go to college, workers in need of retraining—in short, the great majority of the citizenry—must be convinced that the community college is the best place for everyone to fulfill his needs. When breaking down the barriers is stated as an infinite ideal, the difference between the concept of open admissions and the actual enrollment of ever-increasing numbers of people also breaks down.

The colleges' recruiting efforts lead to some rather blatant advertising campaigns, for example, sending a truck complete with posters, blaring music, and college counselors into low-income neighborhoods. These spokesmen actively promote college programs and subtly deny the attractiveness of alternative pursuits. Such antics make it difficult to discern the point at which, "removing the barriers to higher education" becomes "breaking down the sales resistance of the potential client."

Other institutions compete for the people colleges want, the armed services, for example. Note the similarity between the advertisements that say "You can be trained for a higher paying job in the Army" and the recruitment efforts made by the community college vocational and technical program co-

ordinators. The rapidly growing number of continuing studies
and external degree programs operating under university aus-
pices tend also to attract people who might otherwise attend
community colleges. But the prime institutional competitor is
the welfare system. Because welfare agencies and community
colleges provide many similar services they compete for the
same pool of public funds—and clients. (Welfare agencies do
seek and attempt to retain their clientele.)

In addition, young people are beginning to resist affiliation with any institution that exercises a measure of control
over their life. A sizable number try to avoid being influenced
by any bureaucracy, believing instead that alternative pursuits
are at least as rewarding. The magnitude of this phenomenon
is the great unknown that will affect future college enrollments.

Assuming that great numbers of nontraditional students
can be enticed into enrolling, the problem of presenting something useful to them while they are there still remains. However, few colleges staff or operate compensatory programs effec-
tively. College instruction in its present form is the real barrier
to college for low-ability students and for students with personal
goals that differ from the ones other students have. In short,
equal opportunity has not been provided when there has not
been equal opportunity to learn.

Many faculty members recognize this anomaly but are
powerless or confused about how to provide the changed education. Their leaders—both local and national—argue all too
infrequently for the imaginative organizational patterns and instructional procedures that would mitigate the problem. To
date, the campaigns for open admissions have far outstripped
the ability of the institution to place students in appropriate
curriculums and to implement new instructional forms. To be
successful the colleges should maintain a balance between their
efforts to attract new students and their capabilities for placement, instruction, and curriculum development. This has not
happened.

The dilemma generated by postulating infinite ends is
apparent also in the case of social standing. If, as is alleged, college attendance enhances social standing, then open access,

especially if it changes the lines of social stratification, must have a negative effect on certain groups. Who are these groups? What form will their discomfort take? Will those who have positions near the top of the heap lose status? If so, how can they be convinced that egalitarianism is desirable or that no one is reduced if more people enjoy the benefits of exposure to the liberating arts or to job training?

This same question of relative standing impinges on the colleges internally as well. When there is only so much money the number of curriculums and jobs is finite. Which student will willingly give up his position in a desirable program to a new student? Which faculty member or administrator will step aside of his own volition? The AACJC 1971 study of a representative national sample of community colleges revealed some student and staff attitudes pertinent to these questions (Bushnell, 1973). Presidents, instructors, and students were asked to rank a number of college goals in order of preference. The students ranked the statement "Allocate percent of enrollment for minority groups or those of low socioeconomic status" eleventh of twelve goals on the list they were given. Faculty members placed the goal, "Attract representative number of minority faculty members," next to last on their list as well. And the presidents ranked these two goals second and third from last respectively on their list of twenty-six (putting them just ahead of "Strengthen religious faith of students").

These perceptions have given rise to concomitant behavior. One such instance was recounted in *Change* magazine in June 1972: "For the first time the Social Science Division was confronted with a radical group of faculty and students. . . . This group began to contest for power within the Division. The conflict crystallized over the hiring of faculty. . . . When a Princeton PhD with impeccable credentials in East Asian history was passed over while a recent imaginative Richmond College graduate, strongly identified with the New York Latin community but lacking advanced degrees, was enthusiastically hired, the lines were drawn. For the first time tokenism had been replaced by genuine pluralism, and the political balance in the Division was tipping the way of the radical group.

The others had a great deal of difficulty accepting their loss of power." From this incident it seems that unless the institutions can both continue their traditional activities *and* expand sufficiently to add on new programs, additional staff, and new students, either the wave of equal opportunity will break up on the rocks of entrenched interest, or it will wash away many people now in the colleges. Perhaps this is one reason why the promulgators of the infinite goal tend also to promote the establishment of sizable numbers of new institutions.

Some demurrers regarding the removal of all barriers to postsecondary education are seen, but these are usually related to the means. Some commentators argue that because higher education is an expensive commodity, the individuals who benefit should pay—a perennial contention that still has a sizable corps of supporters. They feel that postsecondary education will be realistic only when the recipient calculates its values and balances them against the actual economic cost to himself: it is difficult to think rationally about education as long as someone else is paying for it.

Others argue that a hierarchy of institutions can be as effective in screening people as original exclusion is. Since our society requires certification and credentials, and since the trend is to bar no one from college, the future will see sorting within the institution and sorting on the basis of the kind of institution the student attends. The myth of equal opportunity is well served by allowing everyone to attend a community college, they contend, but the meritocracy is equally well served because of the postentrance sorting and the subsequent questioning of where one went to school.

Those who analyze the prevailing rhetoric are not necessarily antagonistic to the concept of the open door college. Quite the contrary—some of them are among the most fervid supporters of community colleges. For example, John Lombardi, former president of Los Angeles City College, for years has criticized the unbounded claims of the national spokesmen for the community college. Yet his attempts to advance community college education since the 1940s are second to none.

Solving the problem of serving the largest number of

people in the best way is partially a matter of stating the goals in finite terms. Speak of reducing geographic barriers, for example, by placing a college within reasonable commuting distance (approximately thirty miles) of 95 percent of the population, but recognize that these barriers can never be eliminated. Do not attempt to remove all financial barriers but suggest a realistic figure for student support and calculate and publicize the total cost (the GI Bill offers a model for this). Open the door of admission but stop the advertising until some genuine alternatives in curriculum and instruction have been tested and installed so that people with different orientations can still benefit. And above all, admit that college is not for everyone, that we do not know how to teach the potential enrollees who do not learn in traditional ways or who react negatively to classical school contexts.

How much rhetoric is enough? It is one thing to make high-sounding promises in order to gain funding that will allow maintenance of certain necessary levels of service. But if the gap between expectations and realities is a mark of discontent, then community college proponents might well ask how much is added to the general state of social anxiety by promising jobs, higher status, and so on to all matriculants.

Many indicators point to a need for reducing inflated claims. The ecologists suggest the need to reduce ideals of growth in gross national product. The American belief in the virtue of unending inflation in all aspects of life is being challenged. Spokesmen for the community college could set a good example by exercising restraint in their promises. How much better it would be to take the extrinsic forces into consideration by assessing them against a coherent philosophy of education, and, rather than acquiescing to every demand, asking repeatedly, "What are we really trying to do? How does each potential response fit our overall plan? What do we want the college to look like ten or twenty years from now?"

The notion of "community-based education" lures the college leaders on as they ignore the massive efforts of university extension programs and attempt to effect a liaison with the community adult schools.

The colleges would do better to accept the idea of no growth and use the time to improve what they have. The managers of many corporate conglomerates have learned to their sorrow that continuous growth leads eventually to diminishing returns and a lack of institutional flexibility. The repeated calls for a "new mission" are a debilitating diversion.

Bibliography

Entries available through the ERIC Document Reproduction Service (P.O. Box 190, Arlington, Virginia 22210) are indicated by ED (ERIC Document) number. Microfiche price for works under 469 pages: $0.75. Hard copy prices: 1–25 pages, $1.50; 26–50, $1.85; 51–75, $3.15; 76–100, $4.20. For over 100 pages, add $1.20 for each 25-page increment (or fraction thereof). Postage must be added to all orders ($0.18 for the first 60 pages and $0.08 for each additional 60 pages). ERIC documents may also be found on microfiche in more than 400 libraries throughout the country.

ADAMS, S. "Higher Learning Behind Bars." *Change Magazine,* 1973, *5,* (9), 45–90.

ADAMS, S., AND CONNOLLY, J. "Role of Junior Colleges in the Prison Community." *Junior College Journal,* 1971, *41* (6), 92–98.

ASTARITA, S. "Economic Impact in Rural Delaware." "*Community and Junior College Journal,* 1973, *43* (8), 26–29.

ASTIN, A. W., KING, M. R., LIGHT, J. M., AND RICHARDSON, G. T. *The American Freshman: National Norms for Fall 1973.* Los Angeles: American Council on Education, n.d.

ASTIN, H. S., AND BAYER, A. E. "Sex Discrimination in Academe." *Educational Record,* 1972, *53* (2), 101–118.

BALDRIDGE, J. V. "Organizational Change: The Human Relations

Perspective Versus the Political Systems Perspective." *Educational Researcher,* 1972, *1* (2), 4–10.

BARBER, R. *The Importance of Selected Categories of Employee Benefits to Public Junior College Teachers.* Doctoral dissertation, New Mexico State University, 1971. University Microfilms 71-24631.

BARRETT, C. *Relationship Between Perceived Faculty Participation in the Decision Making Process and Job Satisfaction in the Community Colleges of North Carolina.* Doctoral dissertation, North Carolina State University, 1969. University Microfilms 70-9173.

BAYER, A. E. "College and University Faculty: A Statistical Description." *ACE Research Reports,* 1970, *5* (5), 1–48.

BAYER, A. E. "Teaching Faculty in Academe: 1972–73." *ACE Research Reports,* 1973, *8* (2), 1–68.

BEASLEY, W. *Faculty Attitudes Toward the California Community College.* Doctoral dissertation, University of Southern California, 1971. University Microfilms 72-11903.

BEER, M. *Leadership Employee Needs and Motivation.* Ohio State University Bureau of Business Research, Monograph 129. Columbus, Ohio: Ohio State University, 1966.

BENNIS, W. *Who Sank the Yellow Submarine?* Speech delivered at the Wright Institute Conference on Graduate Education in America. Berkeley, Calif., Aug. 31, 1972.

BETTS, L. (Ed.) *Servicemen's Opportunity College Catalog.* Washington, D.C.: American Association of Community and Junior Colleges and the Department of Defense, 1973. 37 pp. (ED 076 191)

BIALEK, H. *The PREP Program at Monterey Peninsula College.* Alexandria, Va.: Human Resources Research Organization, 1971. 12 pp. (ED 055 582)

BLACKBURN, R., AND BYLSMA, D. *Changes in Organizational Structure and in Locus of Decision Making: A Test of Theory in Community Colleges Before and After Collective Negotiations.* Unpublished paper, 1970. 17 pp. (ED 057 791)

BLAI, B., JR. *Values and Perceptions of a Private Junior College Faculty: Public Community College Faculties and Students.* Bryn Mawr, Pa.: Harcum Junior College, 1972. 19 pp. (ED 061 945)

BOGUE, J. P. *The Community College.* New York: McGraw-Hill, 1950.

BRAWER, F. B. *Personality Characteristics of College and University Faculty: Implications for the Community College.* ERIC Clearinghouse for Junior Colleges, Monograph 3. Washington, D.C.: American Association of Junior Colleges, 1968. 104 pp. (ED 026 408)

BRAWER, F. B. *Values and the Generation Gap: Junior College Freshmen and Faculty.* ERIC Clearinghouse for Junior Colleges, Monograph 11. Washington, D.C.: American Association of Junior Colleges, 1971. 77 pp. (ED 050 724)

BRAWER, F. B. *New Perspectives on Personality Development in College Students.* San Francisco: Jossey-Bass, 1973.

BRIGGS, J. W. "Non-Rehiring of Certified Employees." Los Angeles: Office of the County Counsel, 1972.

BROWN, J. W., AND SHUKRAFT, R. C. "Personal Development and Professional Practice in College and University Professors." Unpublished doctoral dissertation, Graduate Theological Union, 1971.

BURNETT, E. "Mobile Classrooms Bring Vocational Education to Rural America." *American School and University,* 1972, *45* (4), 42–44.

BUSHNELL, D. S. *Organizing for Change: New Priorities for Community Colleges.* New York: McGraw-Hill, 1973.

California Education Code. Vol. 1. Sacramento, Calif.: Documents Section, Department of General Services, State of California, 1971.

CAMPBELL, R. "Collective Bargaining: Some Reflections of a President." *Community and Junior College Journal,* 1974, *44* (4), 25–28.

CARL, K. "Rehabilitating the Physically Handicapped: The Williamsport Story." *American Vocational Journal,* 1972, *47* (8), 36–38.

CARLSON, C. "Serving the Needs of Retired Persons." *Community and Junior College Journal,* 1973, *43* (6), 22–23.

The Carnegie Commission on Higher Education. *Carnegie Commission National Survey of Faculty and Student Opinion.* Berkeley, Calif., 1969.

The Carnegie Commission on Higher Education. *Higher Education: Who Pays? Who Benefits? Who Should Pay?* New York: McGraw-Hill, 1973a.

The Carnegie Commission on Higher Education. *Priorities for Ac-*

tion: Final Report of the Carnegie Commission on Higher Education. New York: McGraw-Hill, 1973b.

The Carnegie Commission on Higher Education. *Tuition: A Supplemental Statement to the Report of the Carnegie Commission on Higher Education on "Who Pays? Who Benefits? Who Should Pay?"* New York: McGraw-Hill, 1974.

CARPENTER, M. "The Role of Experimental Colleges in American Higher Education." In W. H. Stickler (Ed.), *Experimental Colleges.* Tallahassee, Fla.: Florida State University, 1964.

CARROLL, B. *Job Satisfaction: A Review of the Literature.* Cornell University Industrial and Labor Relations Library, Key Issues Series No. 3, Feb. 1969.

CASSE, R. M., WAHRER, R., AND ROGERS, J. "Adult Drug Education in a Community College." *Adult Leadership,* 1972, *21* (1), 2–6.

CHAIT, R., AND FORD, A. "Can A College Have Tenure . . . and Affirmative Action, Too?" *The Chronicle of Higher Education,* 1973, *8* (2), 16.

CHANDLER, M. K., AND CHIANG, C. "Management Rights Issues in Higher Education." In M. C. Benewitz (Ed.), *National Center for the Study of Collective Bargaining in Higher Education Proceedings, Annual Conference (1st, April 1973).* New York: Bernard Baruch College, City University of New York, 1973. 135 pp. (ED 086 096)

CHANIN, R. H. *Protecting Teachers' Rights.* Washington, D.C.: National Education Association, 1970.

CHEIT, E. F. *Coming of Middle Age in Higher Education.* New York: McGraw-Hill, 1973.

CHICKERING, A. W. *Education and Identity.* San Francisco: Jossey-Bass, 1971.

COHEN, A. M. *Dateline '79: Heretical Concepts for the Community College.* Beverly Hills, Calif.: Glencoe Press, 1969.

COHEN, A. M. "Technology: Thee or Me? Behavioral Objectives and the College Teacher." *Educational Technology,* 1970, *10* (11), 57–60.

COHEN, A. M. "The Twilight Future of a Function." *The Community Services Catalyst,* 1972, *3* (2), 7–16.

COHEN, A. M. (Ed.) *Toward a Professional Faculty: New Directions for Community Colleges.* 1973a, *1* (1).

COHEN, A. M. *Work Satisfaction Among Junior College Faculty Members.* Paper presented to the Annual Meeting of the

California Educational Research Association, Los Angeles, Nov. 28–29, 1973b. 8 pp. (ED 081 426)

COHEN, A. M., AND ASSOCIATES. *A Constant Variable.* San Francisco: Jossey-Bass, 1971.

COHEN, A. M., AND BRAWER, F. B. *Measuring Faculty Performance.* ERIC Clearinghouse for Junior Colleges, Monograph 4. Washington, D.C.: American Association of Junior Colleges, 1969. 90 pp. (ED 031 222)

COHEN, A. M., AND BRAWER, F. B. *Confronting Identity: The Community College Instructor.* Englewood Cliffs, N.J.: Prentice-Hall, 1972.

COHEN, A. M., AND BRAWER, F. B. *The Rio Hondo Exploratory College, 1970–1974.* Los Angeles: University of California, 1974. 98 pp. (ED 088 547)

COHEN, M. J. *College of the Whole Earth.* ERIC Clearinghouse for Junior Colleges, Topical Paper 27. Los Angeles: University of California, 1971, 26 pp. (ED 055 588)

COHEN, M. J. *A Community Educational Service Network.* Unpublished paper, 1972.

COLE, K. "Golden Oldies: Senior Citizens Go Back to School." *Saturday Review of Education,* 1973, *1* (1) , 41–44.

Collective Bargaining/Professional Negotiations. Olympia, Wash.: Joint Committee on Higher Education, 1973.

COLLINS, C. C. *Financing Higher Education: A Proposal.* ERIC Clearinghouse for Junior Colleges, Topical Paper 10. Washington, D.C.: ERIC Clearinghouse on Higher Education, 1970. 29 pp. (ED 037 206)

Community College of the Air Force. General Catalogue Number 1. Washington, D.C.: United States Air Force, 1973.

Community College Faculty Development. Brief prepared for the American Association of Community and Junior Colleges 1973 Assembly, "New Staff for New Students," Warrenton, Va. Nov. 29–Dec. 1, 1973. 23 pp. (ED 081 411)

A Compilation of Data on Faculty Women and Women Enrolled at Michigan State University. East Lansing, Mich.: Office of Institutional Research, Michigan State University, 1970. 56 pp. (ED 056 630)

CONNOR, A., HOWE, S., AND DAVIS, K. (Eds.) *1973 Community and Junior College Directory.* Washington, D.C.: American Association of Community and Junior Colleges, 1973.

CONSTANTINOPLE, A. "An Ericksonian Measure of Personality Development in College Students." *Developmental Psychology,* 1969, *1* (4) , 357–372.

Current. 1973, *6* (4). (A publication of the Florida Association of Community Colleges.)

"DQU: A New Breed." *Saturday Review of Education,* 1973, *1* (2) , 64.

DUNKLE, M., AND SIMMONS, A. *Anti-Nepotism Policies and Practices.* Unpublished document, 1972. 14 pp. (ED 065 037)

ECKERT, R. E., AND STECKLEIN, J. "Career Motivations and Satisfactions of Junior College Teachers." *Junior College Journal,* 1959, *30* (2) , 83–89.

ECKERT, R. E., AND STECKLEIN, J. *Job Motivations and Satisfactions of College Teachers.* Washington, D.C.: U.S. Office of Education, 1961.

ECKERT, R. E., AND WILLIAMS, H. Y. *College Faculty View Themselves and Their Jobs.* Minneapolis, Minn.: University of Minnesota, 1972.

Educational Programs for the Handicapped. Sacramento, Calif.: California Community College, 1971. 267 pp. (ED 083 978)

ELSNER, P. A. "Evaluation and Assessment of Community Service Programs." In D. A. Morgan (Ed.) , *The Two Year College Student and Community Services.* Rochester, Minn.: Continuing Education and Extension, University of Minnesota, 1974.

EPSTEIN, B. R. "Affirmative Action Versus Preferential Treatment." *National Jewish Monthly,* Jan. 1973.

ERICKSON, E. H. *Childhood and Society.* (2nd ed.) New York: Norton, 1963.

EVANS, A. *Faculty Agreement with the Community College Philosophy as Related to Previous Education and Experience in the Junior College.* Doctoral dissertation, University of California, Berkeley, 1970. University Microfilms 71-20802.

Faculty Collective Bargaining in Postsecondary Institutions: The Impact on the Campus and on the State. Background and Recommendations. Denver, Colo.: Education Commission of the States, 1972. 20 pp. (ED 062 968)

FASTEAU, S. "Development of a Community College Program for Physically Handicapped Students." *Rehabilitation Literature,* 1972, *33* (9) , 267–270.

FIELDS, C. M. "Women Seeking Greater Share of Fellowships." *The Chronicle of Higher Education,* 1972, 7 (12) , 1.

FIELDS, C. M. "More and More Women Turn to Courts to Press Claims on Colleges." *The Chronicle of Higher Education,* 1973, *7* (35), 3.

Financing Postsecondary Education in the United States. Washington, D.C.: The National Commission on the Financing of Postsecondary Education, 1973.

FOGG, P. "Old Sun, New Hope for Canada's Native People." *Community and Junior College Journal,* 1972, *43* (1), 21–23.

FRANKEL, S., ALLISON, E. H., AND GEDDES, C. L. *Case Studies of Fifty Representative Work Education Programs.* Santa Monica, Calif.: System Development Corporation, 1973.

FREEDMAN, M. *The College Experience.* San Francisco: Jossey-Bass, 1967.

FREEDMAN, M. (Ed.) *Facilitating Faculty Development: New Directions for Higher Education,* 1973, *1* (1).

FREEDMAN, M., AND BLOOM, M. "Personal History and Professional Career." *New Directions for Higher Education,* 1973, *1* (1), 29–48.

FREEDMAN, M., AND SANFORD, N. "The Faculty Member Yesterday and Today." *New Directions for Higher Education,* 1973, *1* (1), 1–16.

FREEMAN, J. *Women on the Social Science Faculties Since 1892.* Draft of a speech given at the Political Science Association Conference and University of Chicago Panel on Status of Women, Winter 1969. 14 pp. (ED 041 567)

FREUD, S. *Complete Psychological Works.* (Standard ed.) James Strachey (Trans.) London: Hogarth Press, 1953.

FRIEDMAN, N. *The Public Junior College Teacher in Unified Public School System Junior Colleges: A Study in the Sociology of Educational Work.* Doctoral dissertation, University of Missouri, 1965. University Microfilms 65-9109.

FRIEDMAN, S. *News Release #7466.* Chicago: Office of Public Information, City Colleges of Chicago, Feb. 1, 1974.

GARRISON, R. *Junior College Faculty: Issues and Problems.* Washington, D.C.: American Association of Junior Colleges, 1967. 99 pp. (ED 012 177)

GELSO, C., AND SIMS, D. "Perceptions of a Junior College Environment." *Journal of College Student Personnel,* 1968, *9* (1), 40–43.

GENNARINO, E. *An Analysis of Need Structures and Attitudes Toward Teaching Among Full Time Community College Faculty*

Members. Doctoral dissertation, University of Colorado, 1971. University Microfilms 71-25824.

GERTH, D. R. "Institutional Approaches to Faculty Development." *New Directions for Higher Education,* 1973, *1* (1), 83–92.

GIBSON, F. K., AND TEASLEY, C. E. "The Humanistic Model of Organizational Motivation: A Review of Research Support." *Public Administration Review,* 1973, *33* (1), 89–96.

GLEAZER, E. J., JR. "Preparation of Junior College Teachers." *Educational Record,* 1967, *48* (2), 147–152.

GLEAZER, E. J., JR. "AACJC Approach." *Community and Junior College Journal,* 1974a, *44* (6), 3.

GLEAZER, E. J., JR. "What *Now* for the Community Colleges?" *Community and Junior College Journal,* 1974b, *44* (4), 6–11.

GLENNY, L. A. "State Coordination of Two-Year College Financing: A Necessity." *New Directions for Community Colleges,* 1974, *2* (2), 53–68.

Goals vs. Quotas: Implementing Executive Order 11246 as Amended. Boston: Task Force on Equal Academic Opportunity, Eastern Massachusetts Chapter, National Organization for Women, 1972.

GOLD, B. K. *Survey of California Community College Evening Enrollments. Research Study 72–9.* Los Angeles: Los Angeles City College, 1972. 12 pp. (ED 063 928)

GOLDSTEIN, K. *The Organism.* New York: American Book Company, 1939.

GRANDE, J., AND SINGER, D. *An Assessment of and Design for that Portion of the Education Code Dealing with California Public Community Colleges.* Doctoral dissertation, University of Southern California, 1970. University Microfilms 71-12388.

GREENFIELD, R. "The College Goes to Prison." *Junior College Journal,* 1972, *42* (7), 17–20.

Guide for Financial Assistance and Program Support for Activities in Physical Education and Recreation for Impaired, Disabled, and Handicapped Participants: Foundation Programs. Washington, D.C.: American Association for Health, Physical Education and Recreation, 1973.

GUION, R. M. "Open a New Window." *American Psychologist,* 1974, *29* (5), 287–296.

HAGEN, V. "PREP at Big Bend Community College." *Community and Junior College Journal,* 1973, *43* (5), 22–23.

HALL, W. *A Supplemental Report to the Northeastern California Higher Education Study.* California Rural Consortium and the Coordinating Council for Higher Education Report #72-7A, 1973.

HAMILL, R. E. *The Effects of Teachers in Four-Year Colleges and Universities as Reference Groups for Teachers in Community Colleges.* Doctoral dissertation, University of Oregon, 1967. University Microfilms 68-3984.

HARLACHER, E. L. *The Community Dimension of the Community College.* Englewood Cliffs, N.J.: Prentice-Hall, 1969.

HEATH, S. R., JR. *Personality and Student Development: New Dimensions of Learning in a Free Society.* Pittsburgh, Pa.: University of Pittsburgh Press, 1958.

HELLING, J., AND BAUER, B. "Seniors on Campus." *Adult Leadership,* 1972, *21* (6), 203–205.

HERZBERG, F., MAUSNER, B., AND SNYDERMAN, B. B. *The Motivation to Work.* New York: Wiley, 1959.

Higher Education in New York State: A Report to Governor Nelson A. Rockefeller. Albany, N.Y.: Task Force on Financing Higher Education, 1973.

HORNIG, L. S. *Affirmative Action Through Affirmative Attitudes.* Paper presented at a Conference on "Women in Higher Education," Syracuse, N.Y., Nov. 28, 1972. 18 pp. (ED 076 091)

HULBERT, T. "The Times of Our Lives." *The UCLA Monthly,* 1973, *3* (5), 1–2.

HUNT, F. *The Role of the Faculty in Organization Change in Junior Colleges.* Doctoral dissertation, Stanford University, 1964. University Microfilms 65-6304.

HUTHER, J. W. "The Open Door: How Open Is It?" *Junior College Journal,* 1971, *41* (7), 24–27.

Identification and Accommodation of Disadvantaged and Handicapped Students in Virginia Community Colleges. White Plains, N.Y. Educational Research Services, 1971. 60 pp. (ED 059 707)

IRVING, C. "Minority Hiring Practices in California State U. System Discriminate Against White Men, B'nai B'rith Charges." *The Chronicle of Higher Education,* 1972, 7 (1), 4.

JALKANEN, A. "Aiding in the Abatement of Drug Abuse." *Junior College Journal,* 1972, *42* (7), 26–27.

JENCKS, C., SMITH, M., ACLAND, H., BANE, M. J., COHEN, D., GINTIS, H., HEYNS, B., AND MICHELSON, S. *Inequality: A Reassessment of the Effect of Family and Schooling in America.* New York: Basic Books, 1972.

JUNG, C. G. *Two Essays on Analytical Psychology.* Volume 7. R. F. C. Hull (Trans.) New York: Pantheon Books, 1953.

KELLEY, W., AND WILBUR, L. *Teaching in the Community-Junior College.* New York: Appleton-Century-Crofts, 1970.

KELLY, M. F., AND CONNOLLY, J. *Orientation for Faculty in Junior Colleges.* ERIC Clearinghouse for Junior Colleges, Monograph 10. Washington, D.C.: American Association of Junior Colleges, 1970. 85 pp. (ED 043 323)

KENNELLY, J. R. *Collective Bargaining in Higher Education in the United States: Conceptual Models and a Survey of Incidence and Extent Among Faculty and Supportive Professional Personnel: Summary Report.* Seattle, Wash.: University of Washington, 1972.

KOHLBERG, L. *The Developmental Modes of Moral Thinking in the Years Ten to Sixteen.* Unpublished paper, 1958.

KOILE, E., AND TATEM, D. "The Student Oriented Teacher." *Junior College Journal,* 1966, *36* (5) , 24–26.

KOONTZ, E. D. *The Best Kept Secret of the Past 5,000 Years: Women Are Ready for Leadership in Education. Fastback Series, No. 2.* Bloomington, Ind.: Phi Delta Kappa Educational Foundation, 1972.

KORIM, A. *Older Americans and Community Colleges: A Guide for Program Implementation.* Washington, D.C.: American Association of Community and Junior Colleges, 1974a.

KORIM, A. *Older Americans and Community Colleges: An Overview.* Washington, D.C.: American Association of Community and Junior Colleges, 1974b.

KURTH, E. L., AND MILLS, E. R. *Analysis of Degree of Faculty Satisfactions in Florida Community Junior Colleges: Final Report.* Washington, D.C.: U.S. Office of Education, 1968. 135 pp. (ED 027 902)

LEONARD, G. B. *Education and Ecstasy.* New York: Delacorte Press, 1968.

LEPPALUOTO, J. R. *Attitude Change and Sex Discrimination: The Crunch Hypothesis.* Paper presented before the Western Psychological Association, Portland, Ore., 1972. 11 pp. (ED 071 548)

LESLIE, L. L. *The Trend Toward Government Financing of Higher Education Through Students: Can the Market Model Be*

Applied? University Park, Pa.: Center for the Study of Higher Education, Pennsylvania State University, 1973

LESLIE, L. L., AND JOHNSON, G. P. *Equity and the Middle Class: On Financing Higher Education.* Paper presented to the Seminar on Low Tuition, American Association of State Colleges and Universities. Washington, D.C., Feb. 14, 1974.

LESTER, R. A. *Antibias Regulation of Universities: Faculty Problems and Their Solutions.* New York: McGraw-Hill, 1974.

LEYDEN, R. C. "The Stephens College Program." In W. H. Stickler (Ed.), *Experimental Colleges.* Tallahassee, Fla.: Florida State University, 1964.

LICHTMAN, J. *The Experimental Subcollege.* Washington, D.C.: ERIC Clearinghouse on Higher Education, 1971. 12 pp. (ED 051 437)

LIND, G. C. "Student Charges by Institutions of Higher Education." In K. A. Simon and M. M. Frankel, *Projections of Educational Statistics to 1981–82.* 1972 ed. Washington, D.C.: Department of Health, Education, and Welfare, 1973.

LOEVINGER, J., AND WESSLER, R. *Measuring Ego Development.* San Francisco: Jossey-Bass, 1970.

LOFQUIST, L. H., AND DAWIS, R. V. *Adjustment to Work.* New York: Appleton-Century-Crofts, 1969.

LOMBARDI, J. *Managing Finances in Community Colleges.* San Francisco: Jossey-Bass, 1973.

LOMBARDI, J. "Community Services for the Community Colleges of the Seventies." In D. A. Morgan (Ed.), *The Two Year College Student and Community Services.* Rochester, Minn.: Continuing Education and Extension, University of Minnesota, 1974.

LOMBARDI, J. *Faculty Workload.* ERIC Clearinghouse for Junior Colleges. Topical Paper 46. Los Angeles: University of California, forthcoming a.

LOMBARDI, J. *RIF: Reduction in Force.* ERIC Clearinghouse for Junior Colleges. Los Angeles: University of California, forthcoming b.

MC CLUSKY, H. Y. "Adult, Continuing, and Community Education: The Shape and Promise of the Field." In F. C. Kintzer (Ed.), *National Conference on Community Continuing Education: Alternative Approaches to Responsibility.* Los Angeles: University of California, 1974.

MAC DONALD, G. B. (Ed.) *Five Experimental Colleges.* New York: Harper and Row, 1973.

MC HUGH, W. F. "Faculty Bargaining: Practical Considerations." In T. N. Tice (Ed.), *Faculty Power: Collective Bargaining on Campus.* Ann Arbor, Mich.: The Institute of Continuing Legal Education, 1972.

MC HUGH, W. F., AND O'SULLIVAN, R. *New York Community College Collective Negotiation Contract Survey.* Albany, N.Y.: State University of New York, 1971.

Macomb County Community College. *Minutes, Regular Meeting, Board of Trustees.* Warren, Mich. Feb. 19, 1974.

The Management and Financing of Colleges. New York: Committee for Economic Development, 1973.

MANICUR, A. R. *Status of Professional Women in Higher Education.* Frostburg, Md.: Frostburg State College, 1969. 7 pp. (ED 067 573)

MARTIN, W. B. *Conformity: Standards and Change in Higher Education.* San Francisco: Jossey-Bass, 1969.

MASLOW, A. H. *Motivation and Personality.* New York: Harper and Row, 1954.

Master Plan for Community Colleges in Maryland, 1973–1983. Annapolis, Md.: Maryland State Board for Community Colleges, 1973.

MATTFIELD, J. A. *Many Are Called, but Few Are Chosen.* Paper presented at the Annual Meeting of the American Council on Education, Miami, Oct. 6, 1972. 7 pp. (ED 071 549)

"Meany Urges Labor Federations to Oppose Higher Tuition." *The Chronicle of Higher Education,* 1973, *8* (4), 2.

MEDSKER, L. L. *The Junior College: Progress and Prospect.* New York: McGraw-Hill, 1960.

MEDSKER, L. L., AND TILLERY, D. *Breaking the Access Barriers: A Profile of Two-Year Colleges.* New York: McGraw-Hill, 1971.

MONROE, C. R. *Profile of the Community College: A Handbook.* San Francisco: Jossey-Bass, 1972.

MOORE, J. *The Attitudes of Pennsylvania Community College Faculty Toward Collective Negotiations in Relation to Their Sense of Power and Sense of Mobility.* Doctoral dissertation, Pennsylvania State University, 1970. University Microfilms 71-6342.

MOREY, A. "Junior College Faculty: A New Breed in Higher Education." In J. W. Trent (Ed.), *The Study of Junior Colleges.*

Vol. 1. Washington, D.C.: Department of Health, Education, and Welfare, 1972. 306 pp. (ED 077 507)

MUNDAY, L. A. "A Comparison of Junior College Students in Transfer and Terminal Curricula." In *The Two Year College and the Students: An Empirical Report.* Iowa City, Iowa: The American College Testing Program, 1969. 152 pp. (ED 035 404)

MURTON, C. J., JR. *The Chief Executive's Role in Collective Bargaining.* Paper presented at the American Association of Community and Junior Colleges Forum, Washington, D.C., Feb. 26, 1974.

MYRAN, G., AND MAC LEOD, D. "Planning for Community Services in Rural Community Colleges." *The Community Services Catalyst,* 1972, *3* (2) , 17–28.

Narcotics Information Resource Center. *Newsletter.* Van Nuys, Calif.: Los Angeles Valley College, Nov.–Dec. 1973.

"New California Postsecondary Education Commission Officially Succeeds Coordinating Council for Higher Education on April 1." *University Bulletin,* 1974, *22* (26) , 133.

NOONAN, J. F. "Faculty Development Through Experimentation and Interinstitutional Cooperation." *New Directions for Higher Education,* 1973, *1* (1) , 93-103.

NORDH, D. "The New Woman and the Now College." *Community and Junior College Journal,* 1972, *43* (1), 15 ff.

OGNIBENE, P. "Treating Heroin Addiction." *New Republic,* 1972, *167* (20) , 20–23.

PARK, Y. *Junior College Faculty: Their Values and Perceptions.* ERIC Clearinghouse for Junior Colleges, Monograph 12, Washington, D.C.: American Association of Junior Colleges, 1971. 75 pp. (ED 050 725)

PARKER, C., AND VECCHITTO, D. "A Noncampus System for Vermont." *New Directions for Community Colleges,* 1973, *1* (2) , 27–37.

PARSONS, M. H. *Staff Development: A Gestalt Paradigm.* Hagerstown, Md.: Hagerstown Junior College, 1974.

PATTERSON, R. A. *Career Patterns and Educational Issues: Pennsylvania Community College Faculty.* University Park, Pa.: Pennsylvania State University, 1971.

PETERSON, J. *Community Centeredness and Institutional Adaptability Under State and Local Control: Case Studies of Two Community Colleges.* Doctoral dissertation, University of California, Berkeley, 1969. University Microfilms 70-13136.

PETERSON, R. E. *American College and University Enrollment Trends in 1971.* Ann Arbor: University Microfilms, 1972.

PETRILLO, J. E. "Are Your Employment Practices Legal?" *ERIC Junior College Research Review,* 1971, *6* (3), 1–3. 4 pp. (ED 054 768)

PIETROFESA, J., AND OTHERS. "Twin Valley Farms: A Program for Drug Abusers." *Community and Junior College Journal,* 1973, *43* (5), 30–31.

PIFER, A. *Women in Higher Education.* New York: Carnegie Corporation, 1971. 45 pp. (ED 058 844)

PIFER, A. *The Improvement of Community Life and the Role of Community and Junior Colleges.* Speech to the annual convention of the American Association of Community and Junior Colleges, Washington, D.C., Feb. 24, 1974.

Policies and Procedures for Administrative Personnel. Warren, Mich.: Macomb County Community College, 1973.

POWLESS, R. "Summaries of Presentations Made by Group Discussion Leaders." In D. Morgan (Ed.), *The Rural Low Income Student and the Community College.* Report of a conference sponsored by the Midwest Regional Group of Title III Grantees of the Higher Education Act, Minneapolis, Minn., Nov. 1971. 50 pp. (ED 062 971)

President's Commission on Higher Education. *Higher Education for American Democracy.* New York: Harper and Row, 1947.

President's Progress Report. Harrisburg, Pa.: Harrisburg Area Community College, 1970.

PURDY, L. N. *A Case Study of Acceptance and Rejection of Innovation by Faculty in a Community College.* Doctoral dissertation, University of California, Los Angeles, 1973. University Microfilms 74-11563.

RAFFEL, N. K. *The Women's Movement and Its Impact on Higher Education.* Speech presented at the Annual Meeting of the Association of American Colleges, San Francisco, Jan. 14–16, 1973. 15 pp. (ED 074 886)

Report of Subcommittee on Equal Opportunities for Faculty and Student Women. Minneapolis, Minn.: University of Minnesota, 1971. 18 pp. (ED 056 637)

Report of the Educational Policies Commission. Washington, D.C.: National Educational Association of the United States, 1964.

RICHARDSON, R. C., JR. "A Reaction to the Commission Recommendation." In D. V. Vermilye (Ed.), *The Expanded*

Campus: Current Issues in Higher Education. San Francisco: Jossey-Bass, 1972.

RIESS, L. *Faculty Governance in Turmoil—Who Speaks for the Junior College Professor?* Long Beach, Calif.: Junior College Faculty Association, 1967. 12 pp. (ED 017 250)

RIO HONDO COLLEGE. *Project Proposal: Development of an Experimental College.* Whittier, Calif.: Rio Hondo College, 1970.

RIO HONDO COLLEGE. *Class Schedule.* Whittier, Calif.: Rio Hondo College, Fall 1972a.

RIO HONDO COLLEGE. *General Outline for the Exploratory College.* Whittier, Calif.: Rio Hondo College, 1972b.

RIO HONDO COLLEGE. *Class Schedule.* Whittier, Calif.: Rio Hondo College, Spring 1973a.

RIO HONDO COLLEGE. *Class Schedule.* Whittier, Calif.: Rio Hondo College, Fall 1973b.

RIO HONDO COLLEGE. *Exploratory College Internal Evaluation Report.* Whittier, Calif.: Rio Hondo College, 1973c.

RIO HONDO COLLEGE. *Is Your "Schooling" Interfering with Your Education?* Whittier, Calif.: Rio Hondo College, 1973d.

ROGERS, J. F. "Staffing Our Colleges in the Present Decade." *Teachers College Record,* 1965, *67* (2), 134–139.

ROKEACH, M. *Beliefs, Attitudes, and Values.* San Francisco: Jossey-Bass, 1968.

ROUECHE, J. E., BAKER, G. A., AND BROWNELL, R. L. *Accountability and the Community College: Directions for the 70's.* Washington, D.C.: American Association of Junior Colleges, 1971.

SALMON, P. B. "Are the Administrative Teams and Collective Bargaining Compatible?" *Compact,* 1972, *6* (3), 3–5.

SANFORD, N. *Where Colleges Fail: A Study of the Student as a Person.* San Francisco: Jossey-Bass, 1967.

SANFORD, N. "Academic Culture and the Teacher's Development." *Soundings,* 1971, *54* (4), 357–370.

SANFORD, N. "Foreword." In A. M. Cohen and F. B. Brawer, *Confronting Identity: The Community College Instructor.* Englewood Cliffs, N.J.: Prentice-Hall, 1972.

SANFORD, N. (Ed.) *The American College: A Psychological and Social Interpretation of the Higher Learning.* New York: Wiley, 1962.

SCHLOMING, R. *Academic Senates for Junior Colleges.* Unpublished paper, 1963.

SCHNEIDER, S. "Living with the Agreement." *Community and Junior College Journal,* 1974, *44* (4) , 20–21.

SCHWILCK, G. I., AND MARTIN, W. B. "Danforth's Community College Institute." *New Directions for Community Colleges,* 1973, *1* (1) , 31–39.

SELLS, L. W. *Availability Pools as the Basis for Affirmative Action.* Paper presented at the 44th Annual Meeting, Pacific Sociological Association, Scottsdale, Ariz., May 5, 1973. 10 pp. (ED 077 461)

SHAW, L. C., AND CLARK, R. T., JR. "The Practical Differences Between Public and Private Sector Collective Bargaining." *UCLA Law Review,* 1972, *19* (6) , 867–886.

SHAWL, W. F. *Self-Analysis by Defined Outcomes.* Speech delivered at the California Junior College Association Conference on Improvement of Instruction, Glendale, Calif., Nov. 16, 1972.

SHAWL, W. F. *The Role of the Academic Dean.* ERIC Clearinghouse for Junior Colleges, Topical Paper 42. Los Angeles: University of California, 1974.

SHULMAN, C. H. *Affirmative Action: Women's Rights on Campus.* Washington, D.C.: American Association for Higher Education, 1972.

SIEHR, H. *Problems of New Faculty Members in Community Colleges.* Washington, D.C.: American Association of Junior Colleges, 1963. 78 pp. (ED 013 093)

SIMON, K. A., AND GRANT, W. V. *Digest of Educational Statistics.* Washington, D.C.: National Center for Educational Statistics, 1973.

SIMON, R. J., AND CLARK, S. M. *Preliminary Study of Professional Contributions and Productivity of Women with Doctorates.* Urbana, Ill.: University of Illinois, 1966. 40 pp. (ED 013 458)

SINE, J., AND PESCI, F. "Occupational Education Development in Rural America." *Community and Junior College Journal,* 1973, *43* (8) , 26–28.

SMITH, J. *College Discovery: America's First PREP Program.* New York: Staten Island Community College, 1971, 53 pp. (ED 058 877)

SPENCER, T. *Sources of Income for Community College Capital Outlay 1970–1971.* Little Rock, Ark.: Department of Higher Education, 1972a.

SPENCER, T. *Sources of Income for Community College Current*

Operation 1970–1971. Little Rock, Ark.: Department of Higher Education, 1972b.

SPIEGEL, H. *Sorting Out Community Constituencies.* Unpublished paper, 1972.

SPRENGER, J. M., AND SCHULTZ, R. E. "Staff Reduction Policies." *College Management,* 1974, *9* (5) , 22–23.

Standards for Women in Higher Education: Affirmative Policy in Achieving Sex Equality in the Academic Community. Washington, D.C.: American Association of University Women, n.d.

The Status of Faculty Women at Indiana State University, A Survey. Terre Haute, Ind.: Indiana State University, 1972. 60 pp. (ED 074 994)

TAMBURELLO, G. *Education: A Reciprocal Civic-Military Objective.* Washington, D.C.: U.S. Office of Education, 1969. 10 pp. (ED 034 522)

TURNAGE, M., AND MOORE, R. *Home Craft Days at Mountain Empire Community College Bridge Generation Gap in Mountain Youth's Search for Identity.* Big Stone Gap, Va.: Mountain Empire Community College, 1973. 8 pp. (ED 078 839)

TURNER, C. (Ed.) *A Guide to the Evaluation of Educational Experiences in the Armed Services.* Washington, D.C.: American Council on Education, 1968.

TUSCHER, J., AND FOX, G. "Does the Open Door Include the Physically Handicapped?" *Journal of Rehabilitation,* 1971, *37* (5) , 10–13.

VAN ALSTYNE, C. *Tuition: Analysis of Recent Policy Recommendations.* Paper presented to the Seminar on Low Tuition, American Association of State Colleges and Universities, Washington, D.C., Feb. 14, 1974.

VAN DYNE, L. "A College That Believes in 'Community.' " *Change Magazine,* 1973a, *5* (1) , 52–55.

VAN DYNE, L. "Colleges' White Men Assail 'Preference' for Minorities." *The Chronicle of Higher Education,* 1973b, *7* (18) , 4.

VESELAK, K., ADAMO, T., MORGENSTEIN, M., AND STRONGIN, H. "Nassau Community College and the Drug Problem." *Journal of Drug Education,* 1971, *1* (2) , 195–202.

WATKINS, B. T. "Will It Be Blacks vs. Women for Faculty Jobs?" *The Chronicle of Higher Education,* 1973a, *8* (5) , 1.

WATKINS, B. T. "Student Demands for 'Practical' Education Are Forcing Major Changes in Curricula." *Chronicle of Higher Education,* 1973b, *8* (10) , 2.

WATTENBARGER, J. L., AND SAKAGUCHI, M. *State Level Boards for Community Junior Colleges: Patterns of Control and Coordination.* Gainesville, Fla.: Institute of Higher Education, University of Florida, 1971. 77 pp. (ED 054 770)

WATTENBARGER, J. L., SCHAFER, S., AND ZUCKER, J. D. "Tuition and the Open Door." *New Directions for Community Colleges.* 1973, *1* (2), 57–64.

WEINER, H. *Comparative Psychology of Mental Development.* (Rev. ed.) Chicago: Follett, 1948.

"Where College Faculties Have Chosen or Rejected Collective Bargaining Agents." *Chronicle of Higher Education,* 1974, *8* (35), 24.

"Which Faculty Members Are Satisfied? The Older, the Rural, the Technical, and the Involved." *Community and Junior College Journal,* 1974, *44* (6), 56.

WHITE, B. E., AND WHITE, L. S. *Women's Caucus of the College Art Association Survey of the Status of Women in 164 Art Departments in Accredited Institutions of Higher Education.* New York: College Art Association of America, 1973. 8 pp. (ED 074 901)

WILLIAMS, E. *Faculty Involvement in Policy Formulation in Three Selected Public Community Colleges of Oregon.* Doctoral dissertation, Oregon State University, 1970. University Microfilms 70-14143.

WILMS, W. W. "Proprietary and Public Vocational Students." *College and University Bulletin,* 1974, *26* (7), 3–6.

WILSON, R. C., AND GAFF, J. G. "Student Voice—Faculty Response." *The Research Reporter,* 1969, *4* (2), 1–4.

Work in America. Report of a Special Task Force to the Secretary of Health, Education, and Welfare. Cambridge, Mass.: MIT Press, 1973.

WOZNIAK, L. C. *A Study of the Relationship of Selected Variables and the Job Satisfaction/Dissatisfaction of Music Faculty in Two-Year Colleges.* Doctoral dissertation, The Catholic University of America, 1973. University Microfilms 73-25151.

YOLLES, S. "Student Use of Drugs: Facts and Fables." *The Education Digest,* 1971, *37* (3), 13–16.

ZION, C., AND SUTTON, C. "Integrated Inservice Development." *New Directions for Community Colleges,* 1973, *1* (1), 41–51.

Index